£2.50

KU-132-639

John Nash by Sir Thomas Lawrence, 1827. A portrait in oils presented by Nash to Jesus College, Oxford. Reproduced by permission of the College.

JOHN NASH

The Prince Regent's Architect

TERENCE DAVIS

DAVID & CHARLES
NEWTON ABBOT

0 7153 5959 2

First published in 1966
by Country Life Limited
This edition with corrections
by David & Charles (Holdings) Limited 1973

© Terence Davis 1966, 1973

All rights reserved. No part of this
publication may be reproduced, stored
in a retrieval system, or transmitted,
in any form or by any means, electronic,
mechanical, photocopying, recording or
otherwise, without the prior permission
of David & Charles (Holdings) Limited

Printed in Great Britain by
Redwood Press Limited Trowbridge Wiltshire
for David & Charles (Holdings) Limited
South Devon House Newton Abbot Devon

TO MY FATHER
with affection and respect

Contents

List of Illustrations

HALF-TONE PLATES

DRAWINGS IN THE TEXT

ACKNOWLEDGMENTS FOR ILLUSTRATIONS

Acknowledgments are due to the following for permission to reproduce the photographs and drawings listed below:
Mr M. R. Dudley: Frontispiece; National Monuments Record: 1, 3, 23, 26, 40, Figs. 2–7; National Library of Wales: 4; British Museum: 5, 19, 20, 34, 48, 65, 66; Royal Institute of British Architects: 8–16, 18, 27, 41, Figs. 8, 10, 11; County Borough of Brighton: 21, 37, 72, 73, 74, Fig. 9; Radio Times Hulton Picture Library: 22; Mr Peter Rogers: 24; Mr Edwin Smith: 25; Mr A. Rowan: 28; Ulster Museum: 29; Irish Georgian Society: 30; Commissioners of Public Works in Ireland: 33, 35; Harold C. Tilzey: 36; Messrs Batsford: 38; Mr W. L. C. Baker: 42; Messrs Barratts: 43; Ministry of Works: 52; Mr John McCann: 54; Victoria and Albert Museum: 70; London Museum: 75, 76; *Architect's Journal*: Fig. 1; Mr I. Wynn Jones: Figs. 2–7.

Acknowledgments

HER MAJESTY THE QUEEN has graciously consented to the reproduction of photographs of Buckingham Palace. I am also most grateful to the owners of houses and others for much kindness and hospitality while on research travels and when writing this book; my special thanks in this respect are due to Lord Caledon, Lord O'Neill, Sir Walter Burrell, Bt, Sir Peter Hoare, Bt, the Hon. Desmond Guinness, Mr Marcus Clements, Mr Geoffrey Woolley and Mr John Lewis-Crosby.

I am indebted to Dr Nikolaus Pevsner and Mr Christopher Hussey for guidance on certain aspects of the subject and Mr Clifford Musgrave has kindly answered many queries concerning the Royal Pavilion. Mr John Harris, Mr Desmond Fitz-Gerald, and Mr Alistair Rowan have drawn my attention to material suitable for illustrations. Mr Peter Silsby, Mr Geoffrey Smith-Wyatt and Mrs Hazel Thurston have helped to collate material from various sources and Mr I. Wyn Jones has generously allowed me to use drawings and notes from his thesis on Nash's work in Wales.

I have also received much help from the archivists of the County Record Offices of Carmarthen, Cornwall, Herefordshire, the Isle of Wight and West Sussex and the librarians and staff of the British Museum, the Victoria and Albert Museum, the London Museum, the National Library of Wales, the County Seely Library (Isle of Wight), the William Salt Library (Stafford) and from Mr John Ainsworth of the National Library of Ireland, the Trustees of which have allowed quotations from the Clements Papers.

Several representatives of the Pennethorne family have assisted me in my researches and in particular I have appreciated the co-operation of Mrs Neville Laing, Mr Peter Laing and Mr C. J. Pennethorne Hughes.

My debt to Sir John Summerson is two-fold: the existence of his pioneering *John Nash* has made this book possible and his comments and corrections after reading my manuscript have been of the greatest value.

London, 1966 — Terence Davis

Introduction

WHEN JOHN NASH was born, Wrotham Park in Middlesex had just been completed by Isaac Ware, an architect who, in this instance, had provided the Palladian ideal combined with rococo elements. These elements represented a growing desire to escape from the rigid discipline of (and boredom with) the Orders; it was the end of the purists' Palladianism.

By the time Nash was in his early twenties a house of a very different nature was rising in Herefordshire and although the dying Palladianism of Wrotham would influence his work from time to time, it was Downton Castle that proved to be the constant ancestor of all his schemes. It looked like a medieval castle, but contained Classical rooms of much elegance; its picturesque silhouette belied its sophisticated interior. The plan was unrestricted by four walls and the exterior could be manipulated at will to enclose any number of rooms of all shapes and sizes. Once Nash grasped this principle of free planning he was never to abandon it and even his London works are extensions of the principle; they were convenient shells inside which were concealed anything from an hotel to a terrace of houses, a bank to a retail store, and combinations of many other metropolitan amenities.

When he got into his stride, although he would tackle almost any challenge, Nash had two main things to offer: country houses and townscapes, both rooted in the same romantic idiom. The basic country house formula (showing little development and therefore making chronology less important than geographic or style grouping) contained four common ingredients: a round tower, a long entrance-hall gallery, a spectacular staircase and a loggia or conservatory. These features were sometimes used without success, sometimes with brilliance and represent a development from Neo-classical planning. The townscape formula offered blocks of residential or commercial premises disguised as Classical palaces and so disposed as to produce scenes of great variety. As Nash's career progressed the country houses gave way to the townscapes and it is on these that his fame, if not his reputation as an architect, rests.

Because of his lack of respect for careful detail Nash may have considered himself fortunate to have been born at a time of social change when the *parvenus* were more concerned with overall effect than scholarly detail and when the revolt against strict Palladianism and Neo-classicism was being waged by the leaders of architectural taste. Although his training was Classical he became the champion of this revolt through the doctrine of the Picturesque; a sketchy form of this doctrine suited him very well and he made it his own. He never really understood the Orders or, if he did, he rarely applied them correctly and his critics are therefore largely drawn from the ranks of the precise Classicists. Gothic he understood even less and yet, paradoxically, he combined it with Classical elements in houses of immense charm; and it is partly because these houses are not 'correct' that they are so attractive. They possess all the originality, spontaneity and wit that the later 'authentic' Gothic Revival houses lacked.

Most of Nash's career spanned two financial calamities, one when he was a young and inexperienced speculator in London and the other at his death in the Isle of Wight. His work can be traced and appraised, but the story of his personal life is made threadbare by certain, so far, impenetrable mysteries. The little we do know of his character is consistent and presents a picture of a talented adventurer of relentless drive and determination; but there is no documentation to throw light on these basic mysteries, the solution of which would reveal his true nature and explain the circumstances of several extraordinary turns of fortune. Without doubt his most important commissions were brought about by intrigue at Court and a facility for self-promotion with those who would be most useful. But the vital facts remain in obscurity.

In the early days of his career his commissions were scattered far and wide across England, Wales and Ireland (some still remaining to be identified) until the burden of his London schemes claimed most of his energies. The larger country houses influenced a generation of architects and it is as easy to confuse the Irish houses of the brothers Pain with their master's work as it is the buildings of Decimus Burton and other colleagues and pupils.

Nash's skill in villa and cottage design reminds us that here his influence was not strong enough to discourage the dread tide of ribbon development in the hands of those who understood nothing of the value of relating buildings to their surroundings and vice versa. Nash appreciated the broad principle of this relationship better than any architect had ever done and was given unique opportunities to express it on modest and monumental scales. His country houses and urban planning, seemingly diverse and yet so strangely linked, provide a standard by which his special talents may be judged.

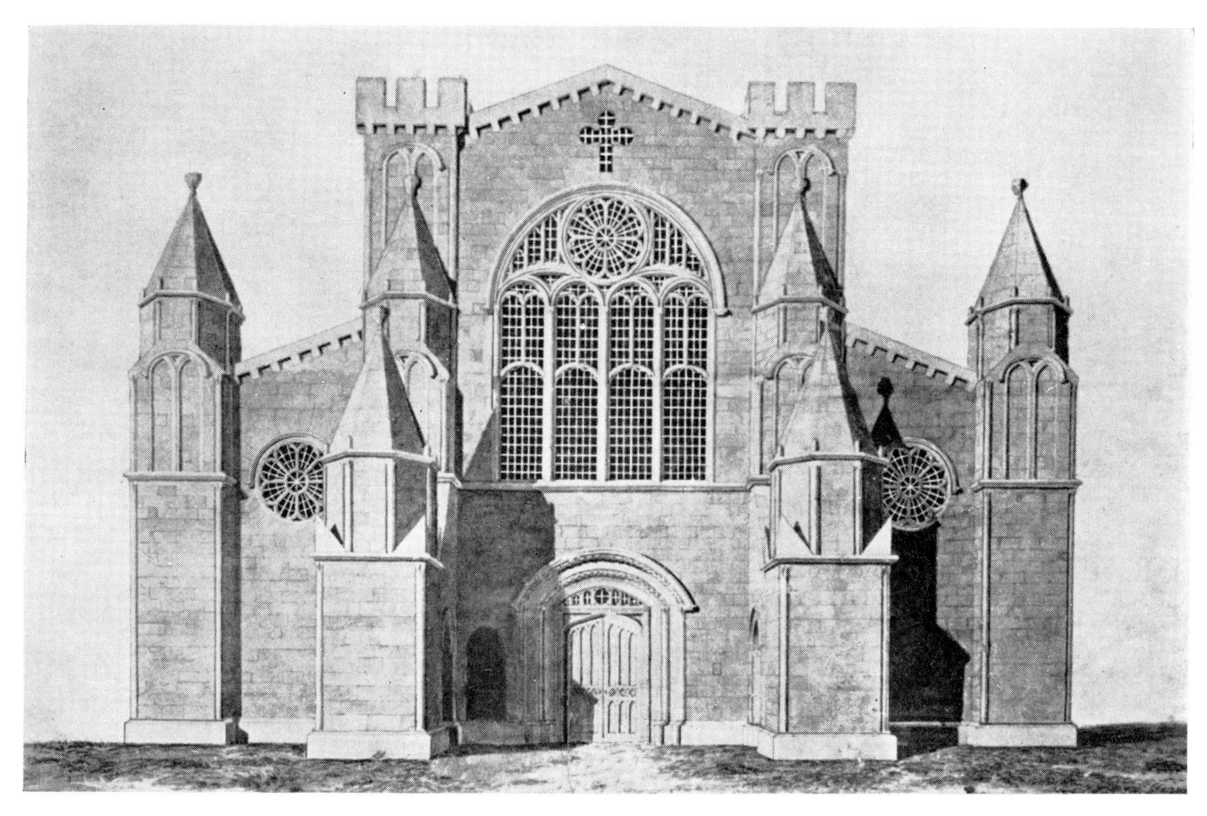

1. St David's Cathedral, the west front: from a drawing by Nash of 1791, in the possession of Mr Cyril Lloyd, L.R.I.B.A.

2. Downton Castle, Herefordshire: built by Richard Payne Knight in 1774. It was the prototype of Nash's castle-Gothic houses.

3. Hafod, Cardiganshire. The house was burnt out in 1807 and Nash's work was destroyed and later replaced by another architect; engraved from a drawing by H. Gastineau, *c.* 1817.

4. Castle House, Aberystwyth, *c.* 1792: the east front. Built for Uvedale Price, this was Nash's first important private commission; from an original drawing in the National Library of Wales, *c.* 1810.

CHAPTER ONE

Retreat to the West

THE first mystery of Nash's life is the place of his birth in 1752. His mother was Welsh and was buried in Carmarthen in 1796, a fact that might help to support Professor Price's theory that he was born at nearby Neath.[1] If this is correct it ties up with a Carmarthen episode of 1828 when Nash was there in connection with the Picton Monument and was called 'our countryman John Nash Esq.'. Neath records show the existence of several Nash families, but no evidence of the architect's birth or baptism can be found; nor at Worcester where he had life-long connections. Without positive evidence, conjecture is profitless and so we must follow Sir John Summerson's belief[2] that he was brought up in Lambeth and that his father was William Nash, a mill-wright, as stated in C. Knight's *English Cyclopaedia* (Biography). No evidence of baptism can be found in Lambeth, but it is established that at a very young age he entered the office of Robert Taylor,[3] the distinguished architect. William Nash died intestate when John (probably the youngest of three sons) was eight, leaving his widow, Ann, with apparently enough money to send the boy later into Taylor's office. William's brother Thomas, however, was a successful calico-printer and a Justice of the Peace with a splendid riverside house at Lambeth, and it is possible that he enabled his young nephew to become an articled pupil to Taylor, the alternative to being employed there in the menial capacity of general office boy.

According to J. Farington's *Diary*[4] and Benjamin Ferrey's *Recollections of A. N. Welby*

[1] Cecil Price: *The English Theatre in Wales in the Eighteenth and Early Nineteenth Centuries*: University of Wales Press, 1948. The author refers to a note by J. Deffett Francis, a local bibliophile, scribbled in one of the books he presented to the town of Swansea which reads: 'His (Nash's) sister, who was the very image of him, sold penny pies in Bridgwater, Som., and told me they were both born in Neath.'

[2] John Summerson: *John Nash*; London, 1935, reprinted 1949.

[3] 1714–88.

[4] J. Farington: *Diary* (edited by J. Greig) 8 vols, 1922–28. Vol. VIII, p. 300.

Pugin (1861), Nash was the reverse of Taylor's champion, and considered his master to be little more than a dullish, plodding practioner of no outstanding merit. In fact, Taylor was the author of many distinguished buildings including Harleyford Manor, Great Marlow, Ely House, Dover Street, London, Grafton House, Piccadilly, Stone Buildings, Lincoln's Inn, and extensive additions to the Bank of England. At one time he and Paine shared all the most important commissions going and his talents were rewarded by knighthood in 1782 on his election as Sheriff of London, six years before his death. His work was as sound and scholarly as much of Nash's was to be slip-shod and light-weight.

Nash seems to have worked with Taylor for about ten years—from 1767–78—and we may assume that he was concerned with some of his master's notable London commissions as draughtsman and assistant. He would have learnt to recognise the correct use of Classical detail and the discipline required to design in the waning and diluted Palladian style. His private commissions of any size were to show traces of this discipline and early training and it was not until he was re-planning the great new streets of London that he threw careful Classical detail to the winds. But during his apprenticeship Nash was being influenced by Taylor's work and by the work of Sir William Chambers, whose vast rebuilding of Somerset House was rising on the north bank of the Thames. He would also be familiar with the great complex of buildings at Greenwich where coupled columns—later to be his favourite device for colonnades—stood in endless ranks. His store of references was increasing from many sources; from great masters of the past, from his 'dull' old master and from those whose greater and more original talents were working in London at the time.

But Nash was impatient, ambitious and longing to leave Taylor's office to try his wings in the world outside. All he needed was an excuse to leave and this was provided in 1778 when his rich Uncle Thomas died in Paris. (His remains were placed in a splendid marble mausoleum at Farningham, possibly designed by the student-architect).[1] As if to prove that John was the favourite nephew, he was left a legacy of £1,000 (a considerable sum in those days), his mother received a small allowance and his brothers £100 a year. Perhaps Nash had once confided to his uncle that he wanted to invest a lump sum in London property and from there to found an architect-builder's fortune. The accent would have been on 'builder' for Nash was born with an insatiable desire to control every aspect of a project. Architecture was only a part of his thinking; the rest belongs to a much wider field, that of property speculation. Architecture was all very well, but building and planning were much more rewarding exercises and, as we shall see, a larger part of his creative nature.

Until Uncle Thomas died we assume that Nash lived in Lambeth, but upon receiving his £1,000 legacy he proceeded to invest it in a property in Bloomsbury.[2] How he came to

[1] *See* sketch, Summerson: *op. cit.*, p. 24.

[2] *See The Architect and Building News*, 7th December, 1934, and papers in the Bedford Estate Office.

choose this area is not known, but at the time it was a fashionable neighbourhood and a highly suitable springboard from which to launch any property ventures. It promised to be a lucrative investment as, in fact, the property comprised several houses in one—No 17, Bloomsbury Square, 23 and 24, Great Russell Street and two smaller houses to the west. When Nash bought them in about 1778 the larger houses were brick and of early 18th-century date. He proceeded to cover the walls with stucco, rusticate the ground floor and add giant Corinthian pilasters to the Bloomsbury Square façade. Thus, in one flamboyant gesture, he transformed these plain houses into a stuccoed mansion. There was nothing like it in London and it portended the great stretches of plastered terraces and street architecture to come.

Fig. 1. 17, Bloomsbury Square, London, *c.* 1778, as it appeared before later alterations. Now the premises of The Pharmaceutical Society.

Naturally the building had its critics, not the least of whom was the neurotic Soane,[1] who was to become Nash's permanent rival though the grudges were, owing to his peculiar nature, mostly on Soane's side. But, worse than criticism, the building was a financial disaster. In October, 1783, Nash was declared bankrupt and at the age of thirty-one had to start all over again, his little fortune gone.

It is reasonable to suppose that on her allowance from Uncle Thomas Nash's mother spent her last years in her native Wales where she died. Nash must have joined her there in 1784 for the next we hear of him is in partnership with someone named Saxon, a builder-carpenter of Carmarthen, and together they won the tender of six hundred guineas for re-roofing and providing a new ceiling for St Peter's Church, Carmarthen, after a fire. He

[1] Summerson: *op. cit.*, p. 26.

had escaped from the slur of his London failure and was starting to build a new reputation for himself in Wales.

Carmarthen was a typical small Welsh market town during the 18th century and enjoyed some importance and prosperity because it was a small river port and also on the coaching road. It served a large agricultural area and returned its own Member to Parliament. At this time the two main buildings were the rather unimpressive church of St Peter, a dull perpendicular church, and a town hall. Its lack of architectural laurels was partly compensated for by its pleasant position above the River Towy and its beautiful surrounding hills and countryside; and in the countryside lived several squires of great wealth and influence.

Nash continued his association with Saxon for some while, and W. Spurrell in his *Carmarthen and its Neighbourhood* (1779) attributes several buildings in the town to Nash. At the end of the 18th century the town was growing rapidly and Nash may have been concerned with several small houses of no great distinction. He is said to have built a public house called the 'Six Bells' near the church and Jeremy's Hotel—a building of some charm with a bow front and a narrow Gothic window at the rear running up three storeys. He built a modest house for himself known as 'Green Gardens'. It was a building of no special character and it remains to this day. In 1787 he leased from the Corporation a piece of low-lying land on which was situated a lime kiln and later he bought a large piece of woodland. It therefore seems that he was speculating once more in order to supplement his earnings from the small but possibly lucrative jobs that came his way in and around Carmarthen, and this experience was to hold Nash in good stead later when a practical knowledge of property development was to be so valuable. A former co-pupil in Sir Robert Taylor's office now appeared on the scene; he was S. P. Cockerell,[1] already a successful architect and two years Nash's junior. No doubt their meeting provided a further spur to Nash's ambitions. At no time did he see himself as a large fish in this small pool; the pool would have to be large too and he always had an eye to the socially (and thereby professionally) influential friend. He did not know the meaning of social barriers and his completely uninhibited personality was welcomed and appreciated by nine out of ten. He always thought himself welcome and he usually was. People of standing cast a blind eye to his lack of reserve because they were amply compensated by his amusing ways, wit and originality. His appearance fitted his personality; it was pugnacious and thrusting. He was short and bullet-headed with features that were at once both undistinguished and irresistible. Though portraits of him in later years endow his features with a semblance of dignity and learning, mischievous humour is always there. Even in the somewhat Voltaire-like marble bust of 1831 by William Behnes,[2] a good-natured expression emerges. It is the

[1] He was building Middleton Hall, near Carmarthen, at this time. *See* p. 23.

[2] The original is in the possession of Mr Peter Laing, of Corton Denham House, Dorset, descendant of Sir James Pennethorne. There is a plaster copy at the R.I.B.A. and another copy is to be found on a bracket

face of a man who took success and failure in his stride. Mrs Arbuthnot writing in her journal[1] in 1824 said that he was 'a very clever, odd, amusing man with a face like a monkey's but civil and good-humoured to the greatest degree'. Two years earlier Nash had described his own 'thick, squat, dwarf figure, with round head, snub nose and little eyes . . .',[2] thus providing in a few words a picture of physique and personality.

It was undoubtedly this mixture of bombast and self-effacement that endeared him to many in these early, rather dim, Carmarthen days and that would soon lead to commissions of considerable importance.

It was in 1792 that Nash finished work as the designer of Carmarthen Gaol, the first important work of his career. If one does not readily associate the great Nash of Regency London with anything as dismal and uncompromising as a gaol, we must remember that for a virtually unknown builder to be commissioned to design an important civic building was, even in remote Carmarthen, an honour and one which Nash readily took. Moreover he went on to design two further gaols—one in Cardigan[3] shortly afterwards and another in Hereford in 1794–96. The latter was a more sophisticated design from a more experienced architect and showed Nash experimenting with Greek Doric columns, semi-circular grilled windows, heavy rustication, pediment and cupola.[4]

We do not know who introduced Nash to the Carmarthen Gaol commission, but at this stage of his career it is more useful to consider the design itself rather than how the commission came about. The building has been demolished, but a drawing of it in its original state shows it to be of suitably severe aspect and according to Summerson owes something to Sir Robert Taylor's design for the Middlesex House of Correction in Coldbath Fields.[5] Nash was obviously narrowly confined by functional necessities and there is little if anything to suggest that he was the author. It might be a fairly imposing design from the hand of any reasonably articulate architect-builder of the day. Nash's own handwriting was yet to appear. On touring Wales in 1796, Sir Christopher Sykes remarked: 'The town (Carmarthen) is the most considerable I have seen in Wales. The approach is over a narrow bridge up a steep hill on which the town and castle stand; the latter is entirely new modelled into a new county prison and house of correction, and is convenient, clean and airy. The church is newly repaired.' Thus both Nash's works were admired; and in 1824 when, as a celebrated architect of seventy-six, he visited Carmarthen for probably

on the façade of the small house attached to the southern end of Chester Terrace, Regent's Park. A larger copy in stone by Cecil Thomas was placed under the portico of All Souls', Langham Place, in 1956.

[1] *The Journal of Mrs Arbuthnot*, 1820–32 (edited by F. Bamford and the Duke of Wellington, 1950), entry for 29th August, 1824.

[2] Letter from Nash to Soane of 18th September, 1822, quoted in full, p. 90.

[3] It was smaller than Carmarthen Gaol and of much grimmer appearance. It has been demolished, but sketches from old photographs can be seen in Summerson: *op., cit.* p. 37.

[4] A print of the main elevation is in Hereford Public Library.

[5] *See* Summerson: *op. cit.*, p. 36.

the last time, the Common Council voted £35 for an 'Honorary Gold Box laid in Oak' as a presentation in recognition of his 'Valuable Services'.[1] Without doubt, Nash was highly esteemed in Wales.

In 1793 a subscription of nearly £2,000 was raised to repair the west front of the cathedral at St David's and Nash was asked to make his recommendations. The west front was leaning out under the pressure of the Norman arches within and Nash had to take down the major portion of it and rebuild it.

This involved a new design for the whole front and here Nash produced one of his first known and, alas, crudest essays in Gothic. His well-known cry from the heart, 'I hate this Gothic style; one window costs more trouble in designing than two houses ought to do',[2] is well demonstrated at St David's. But a certain draughtsman who would take all this troublesome detailing off his hands for many years was about to arrive on the scene and work on the St David's elevations. The west window tracery was a hybrid design of inarticulate Gothic-cum-Norman supported by a jumble of buttresses. The whole front was replaced by Sir George Gilbert Scott when the cathedral was restored in 1862. At this time Nash also built a much criticised Chapter House incorporating the 16th-century grammar school, now demolished. The work at St David's was to be an unhappy and long-drawn-out affair. Nearly twenty years later Nash was applying to the Chapter for back-payment of £500 and forty-six years later still Gilbert Scott reported that Nash's work had 'greatly shattered the pillars, arches and superstructure'.[3]

But when work on the cathedral was finished Nash had more interesting things to think about as he had been asked by the people of the small Welsh town of Abergavenny to make his recommendations for improving the Market Place. The commission came via John Vaughan, a very influential landowner and local Member of Parliament (for whom Nash had designed a bathroom in his house, Golden Grove), and entailed the designing of a Market House, new paving and drainage. Also included were 'Butchers Shops, Shops, Sheds, Stalls, and Shambles and other conveniences that shall be judged proper according to a plan and estimate to be delivered in by Mr Nash'.[4] One imagines that this work, modest though it was, gave Nash his first appetite for town planning and schemes that involved more than designing a mere building. But more important still, the work kept him in close contact with John Vaughan and another useful member of the local squirearchy, J. G. Philipps of Cwmgwili—a Whig member for the Borough of Carmarthen.

For several years Nash carried on a voluminous correspondence with Philipps concerning local Whig politics,[5] urging the latter to be less slothful in rallying to the cause and

[1] Order Book, Carmarthen.

[2] Kenneth Clark: *The Gothic Revival*, 1928, p. 153.

[3] Gilbert Scott's report to the Chapter, 1862.

[4] Abergavenny MSS.

[5] The Cwmgwili Papers, preserved and scheduled in the Carmarthen Library, show that Nash was on intimate terms with Philipps as architect, political adviser and personal friend.

later sending him the London gossip connected with the Party. It is no doubt through these activities that Nash was to come into contact with Charles James Fox, friend of the Prince Regent and leader of a coterie of cultured Whigs, among whose serious interests were the arts, embracing architecture and landscape gardening. Whether he knew it or not, Nash's Whig activities in Wales were stepping stones of the highest importance.

During the summer of 1795 Nash stayed with Sir Edward Winnington at Stanford Court, Worcestershire. While there he discussed Sir Edward's plan to replace the broken stone bridge across the Teme with one made of cast-iron. Nash also had something to do with a cast-iron bridge at far-flung Sunderland and arrived at Stanford as 'the ingenious architect who had built the famous bridge at Sunderland'. But it is possible that Nash claimed authorship having merely given superficial advice to designer and builder. Some years later Lord Glenbervie wrote in his journal:[1] 'Last night I had a long history from Mr Nash of the erection of Sunderland Bridge, which, according to him, was first projected by himself and the design stolen from him by Mr Burdon.' Whatever the facts, Nash was considered a suitable man to design the Stanford bridge and it was described as 'a most light and elegant thing'. Within a matter of hours of completion the bridge collapsed—but apparently in the most gentle manner as a small boy who was on it at the time escaped unhurt. Two years later the bridge had been reinstated and survived for over a hundred years.

On returning to Wales Nash was now in a position to start employing specialised craftsmen in his rapidly expanding business. He advertised for a draughtsman by stating that 'the services of a foreigner would be preferred'. By foreigner Nash hopefully meant French as he always showed a preference for anything French and was to visit Paris several times during his life. By some stroke of fortune a refugee from the Revolution, Auguste Charles de Pugin, arrived in Wales after a swim across the Seine and a boat trip from Rouen. Nash took him on and he became an excellent draughtsman with a liking for Gothic detail and with a special ability to produce appealing colour 'perspectives' from which clients could get a good idea of what a proposed scheme would look like. He was responsible for the working drawings for St David's from which an exhibition was arranged by Nash in 1795 at the Society of Antiquaries, Burlington House. Some of the drawings were by John Adey Repton of whom we shall hear more. The antiquaries expressed 'admiration of the curiosity and singularity of the drawings'.[2] Pugin and his employer became close friends and their association lasted long after Pugin had set up on his own as a water-colourist and draughtsman of considerable distinction. He shared Nash's love of amateur theatricals (a trait in the architect's character that expressed itself in

[1] *The Glenbervie Journals*, 1811, edited by W. Sichel, p.149. Quoted in A. T. Bolton: *The Portrait of Sir John Soane, R.A.*, 1927.

[2] MSS; Society of Antiquaries. The drawings are at Burlington House.

everything he did, everything he created, when given the chance), and together they devised plays and other entertainments and collaborated with Charles Mathews,[1] a talented actor-producer who headed a small company in Carmarthen. In 1796 the Carmarthen Theatre presented *The School for Scandal* and *The Farm House*. In *The School for Scandal*, Nash played Sir Peter Teazle and Mathews called his performance 'admirable'.[2] In the cast and audience were many local personalities through whose offices Nash had built up his Welsh practice.

But, by now, Nash was preparing for a much more important performance—his return to London.

Before we follow Nash back to London we should look at the houses he built for several members of the landed gentry in south Wales. 1787 was the year in which John Vaughan gave him 'a Rouleau of guineas' for designing his bathroom at Golden Grove.[3] From that moment he never looked back and one commission led to another. As we have seen, Vaughan was a powerful local squire and it was through him that Nash was introduced to work worth considerably more than a rouleau of guineas and to people who were to influence his entire outlook on architecture. One person in particular was Thomas Johnes of Hafod. Nash had added a theatrical Palladian front to a forlorn old farmhouse at Dolaucothi[4] owned by a cousin of Johnes and, no doubt, it was through his work there that he went to Hafod—perhaps in its day the most romantic, haunting house in all Wales. The story of Hafod has been told many times[5] and its situation in the remote and tranquil valley of Ystwyth was one of matchless beauty and strange magic. The house was designed in 1783 by Baldwin of Bath for an owner who was not only a soldier, politician, author and agriculturalist but also, more important to our story, an enthusiastic exponent of an ideal that was to affect country house design for many years. The ideal was manifested in the Picturesque—a theory evolved from the belief that buildings and their surroundings should be related in a way quite different from that hitherto considered. It was at Hafod that Nash must have heard Johnes and Richard Payne Knight, his cousin of Downton Castle, Herefordshire, and others discussing how the theory should be put into practice; of how buildings and surroundings alike should show 'movement' and 'irregularity'; of how nature could be encouraged to suit buildings and buildings be made part of nature; of how

[1] His *Life of Charles James Mathews*, an autobiographical work was edited by Charles Dickens in 1879. His son Charles later joined Nash's London office. (*see* p. 104.)

[2] *Ibid.*

[3] Farington: Vol. VIII, p. 301.

[4] The house has fallen into decay, but the parkland is preserved by the National Trust.

[5] Sir James Edward Smith: *A Tour to Hafod, Cardiganshire*, 1810, gives a gentleman tourist's view of the place; Elizabeth Inglis-Jones: *Peacocks in Paradise*, 1950, relates with great feeling for atmosphere the life of Johnes and his family on the estate.

great Italian painters of the 17th century showed these trends; of how English Palladianism should be replaced by something less formal, more flexible, more *romantic*. . . . Thus the Romantic Movement of the 19th century was being born and the style of architecture that obviously fitted best was Gothic; not academic, precise Gothic but something, even if less 'correct', that had a quality of wildness and mystery about it. But the Picturesque Theory was no mere sentimental appreciation of the visual aspects of buildings and their surroundings; it had more profound roots and embraced a serious attempt to combine romantic outline with the practical necessities of modern planning.[1] Nash was to become the greatest exponent of the theory. Knight was to crystallise the whole aesthetic of the Picturesque in a series of letters and essays written between 1794 and 1805, but Johnes's 'essay' was to be Hafod and Nash was there to help and learn. It is almost certain that he added a great octagonal Gothic library in 1793 and he certainly made other alterations to the house. After a disastrous fire in 1807 Johnes wrote '. . . the outward walls are standing and I hope will serve. All Nash's buildings are gone'.[2] The house has now vanished and only a few stones remain to remind us of the earthly paradise that was Hafod.[3]

Although it cannot be dated precisely, Nash's first commission to design a complete house came about this time. It was for Uvedale Price, a neighbour of Payne Knight in Herefordshire, who were both authors of essays on the Picturesque;[4] but it was no ordinary commission as Price was no ordinary client. It was also Nash's first experiment in relating a building to its surroundings, for it was a summer residence of very odd appearance standing on the wild coast of Aberystwyth and became known as Castle House. It was, in fact, a stuccoed villa in Gothic style, the plan triangular in order to exploit the views of coastline in three directions. Nash may have based his plan on Middleton Hall for there the plan is also triangular but with round towers at the corners, whereas Nash's were octagonal. Ranges of rooms linked the towers and a canopied balcony was a prominent feature on the main elevation. The appearance was intended to be in keeping with the rugged landscape, an ideal which must have been difficult to convey in stucco.[5] The villa has long disappeared, but its very conception was an important moment in the development of Nash's initiation into Gothic house design.

[1] Christopher Hussey: *The Picturesque*, 1927, is the fullest account of the theory; articles by the same author discuss the theory in relation to houses described in several issues of *Country Life*.

[2] Cumberland MSS, British Museum.

[3] There is a fine water-colour entitled *Hafod* in the Lady Lever Art Gallery, Port Sunlight. This appears to be an imaginary view of the house, the details in no way resembling the house shown in the engraving of *c.* 1815 when Johnes had rebuilt after the fire.

[4] In 1794 Knight addressed a poem to Price entitled *The Landscape* and in the same year Price published his *Essay on the Picturesque*. Both extol the virtues of the romantic approach to landscape, although they did not agree on all points. *See* N. Pevsner: 'Richard Payne Knight' (*The Art Bulletin*, College Art Assoc. of America; December, 1949, Vol. XXXI, No 4).

[5] Royal Worcester made a china model of the villa.

By now Nash was very busy indeed and, in contrast to Price's eccentric villa, the remainder of his Welsh works are all Classical and were built in the crowded years 1792–1794. Sion House, Tenby, was another architectural freak and was probably built about 1792 when Nash was busy with St David's Cathedral, since the owner, William Routh, a printer of Bristol,[1] had handled Nash's specification for the restoration. It had in common with other of his Welsh houses a basically square plan, but at Sion House there were

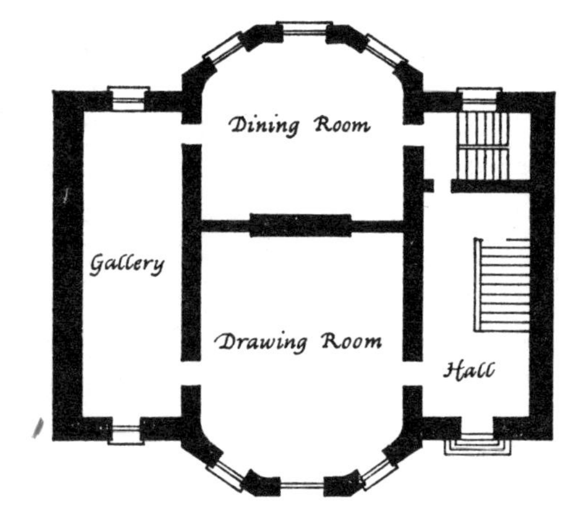

Fig. 2. Sion House, Tenby, *c.* 1792: entrance elevation and ground floor plan.

projecting bows on both main elevations. It was, in fact, a four-storey house of 18th-century character but with the windows of each storey of the same height, thus giving a faintly continental appearance to the composition. The house was built on a prominence and the lowest floor, level with the carriage-way, contained the cellars and kitchens adding to the already unusual proportions of the building. The ground floor plan was unlike anything that Nash designed in Wales and must be attributed to the special requirements of the

[1] Bristol Directories, 1775, *et seq.*

client. The staircase hall was contained to the right of the central bow, the dining and drawing rooms occupying the central portion and giving into a gallery running the whole depth of the house, lit only by windows at each end. Sion was probably named after Sion Downs some miles to the west; it was enlarged and much altered in appearance in the 19th century and destroyed by fire in 1936.

At the time he was employed at Hafod he was also building Ffynone, situated on a hill near Boncath, Pembrokeshire. The owner was a Captain Colby, a friend of Thomas Johnes, and the commission probably came through the latter's introduction. The house is square in plan as were three other of the early houses and originally presented four identical Palladian façades, the outbuildings and service wing being concealed by shrubbery to preserve the four-square simplicity. Each façade was surmounted by a pediment with broad

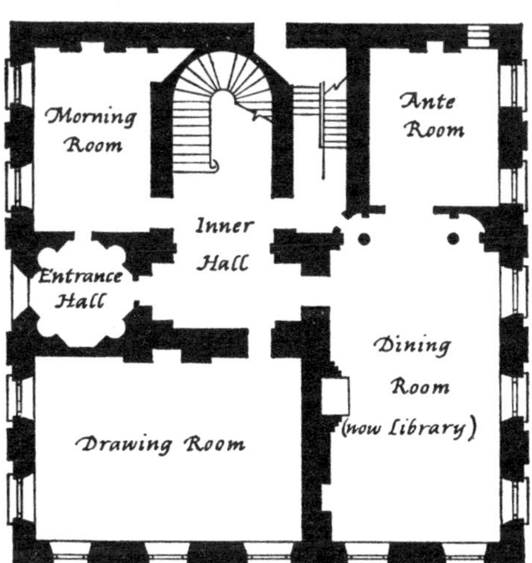

Fig. 3. Ffynone, Pembrokeshire, *c.* 1793: south elevation and ground floor plan.

timber eaves forming deep tympana (derived from Inigo Jones's St Paul's, Covent Garden, and to be used by Nash repeatedly) pierced by a curve-topped window. The ground floor sash windows were set in round-headed recesses divided by Tuscan pilasters. A string course was formed in one continuous line at first floor window sill level. Mr I. Wyn Jones has suggested that Nash may have been influenced by Holywell House, St Albans, sometimes attributed to Sir Robert Taylor, with which it has certain features in common.

Inside, however, we see for the first time, in plan, detail and decoration, an original Nash interior; one which he was to use in the future in a variety of ways and on different scales. The plan is developed round a central hall leading from a vestibule, thence to a semi-circular staircase, the main rooms being disposed around these features. The vestibule or outer hall has simple plaster octagonal vaulting, but the ceiling of the central hall is radially fluted in high relief, an effective refinement he was to introduce successfully at Southgate Grove, London, on a larger scale in 1797. The two halls are divided by a rectangular opening containing a circular fanlight—an unusual feature which is repeated over the front door. The first floor landing also contains carefully detailed plasterwork carried out by a local man, John Watkins. Earlier Nash had taken on a Mr George as a clerk in his office and it was he who acted as clerk of works at Ffynone. Tradesmen's bills and Nash's surveys are preserved in the National Library of Wales and it is interesting to note that for decorating the ceilings, Watkins was paid as follows: 'All roses in coffers, cast and put up, not exceeding 2″ diameter: 1d Each.'[1] George measured and valued all the plasterwork until 1798 when the building was presumably completed and Nash was about to leave the Welsh scene; he then set himself up as an architect in Carmarthen and was employed by the Clerk of the Peace of Cardiganshire to complete Nash's Gaol at Cardigan.

As in most of his later houses, Nash made his main feature the staircase and the one he provided at Ffynone was the forerunner of several. It was built of Painswick stone to Nash's design by a William Drewitt of Bristol and cantilevered from the wall. The S-shaped iron balusters were to become Nash's favourite design and he was to use them even on staircases lit by Gothic windows.

In 1828 the entrance front of Ffynone received a face-lift; although the attractive symmetry of the house was banished, it is possible that Nash himself was responsible for this 'improvement' which consisted of adding a forebuilding in Greek Doric style containing some faintly Gothic detail and enlarging one of the front rooms. (Nash returned to Wales at this time in connection with the monument outside Carmarthen: a Doric column, the base surrounded by military trophies, and surmounted by a figure of General Picton of Waterloo fame.[2]) In 1904 the whole spirit of Nash's Ffynone disappeared in a drastic

[1] Spence-Colby MSS, National Library of Wales, Aberystwyth.

[2] The foundation stone was laid by Lady Dynevor in 1825 and the monument, built of limestone at a cost of £3,000, was completed in 1827.

exterior remodelling by Inigo Thomas, the interior alone remaining, as it still does, intact.[1]

Another house that suffered an even more grotesque fate is nearby Llysnewydd at Henllan Bridge. When built for Colonel Lewes, shortly after Ffynone, it was clearly not only a house of great charm, but also one where Nash had developed and perfected the Ffynone plan. Today even the most hawk-eyed architectural scholar would find it difficult

Fig. 4. Llysnewydd, Henllan Bridge, *c.* 1794: garden elevation and ground floor plan.

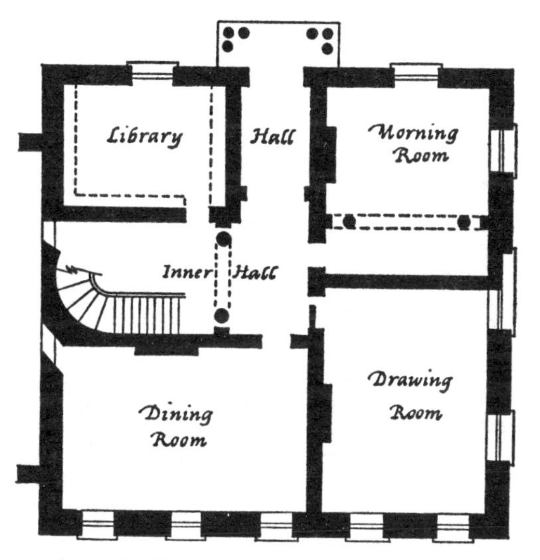

to detect the hand of Nash under its heavy shroud of Victorian ironmongery. The general shape remains the same—square—but the well-spaced fenestration has been entirely changed and a balcony, supported on a mixture of giant Ionic and thin cast-iron columns, now cuts the main elevation in two. The attic storey, a feature not concealed by a parapet or balustrade, consisted of three oval windows (now replaced by rectangular ones) set in panels divided by short pilasters. This is the first instance we see of Nash's oval windows,

[1] *See* illustrations of the interior in Terence Davis: *The Architecture of John Nash*, 1960.

but they were to reappear often throughout his career from Llysnewydd to Southgate; from Cronkhill in Shropshire to Sandridge in Devon and back; and later, to Carlton House Terrace. The interior of Llysnewydd has also been massacred and only the dome raised on a fluted drum, to light the now vanished semi-circular staircase, and also the library with its fitted bookcases, remind us that Nash was ever there.[1]

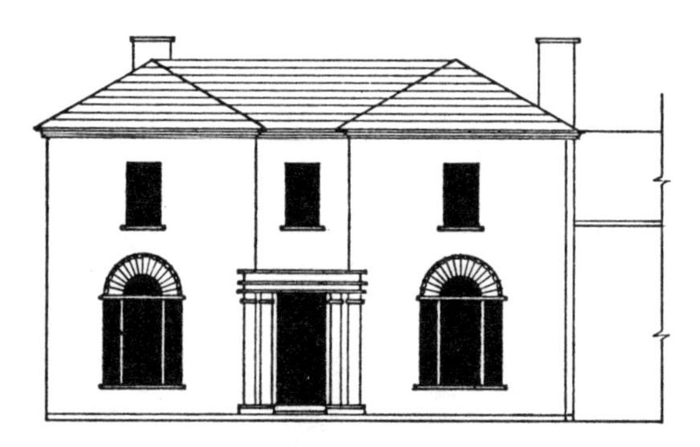

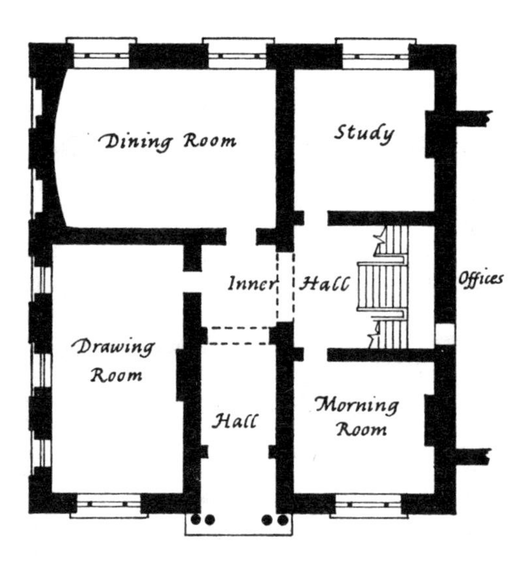

Fig. 5. Llanayron, Aberayron, *c.* 1794: entrance elevation and ground floor plan.

Llanayron, near Aberayron, built also about 1794, for Major Lewis (no relation of Lewes of Llysnewydd although the two families were linked by marriage in 1812) is again square in plan. It is a severely plain stuccoed house with no pediments, pilasters or attic storey and has escaped 'improvement'. It relies for its success on well-spaced fenestration, the windows being set in shallow arched recesses. Each of the Palladian windows in the east and west elevations are, however, surmounted by Adamesque semi-circular tympana containing radial flutes, the only suggestion of 'decoration' in the whole building. Used

[1] *Ibid. See* illustrations before and after alterations to the exterior.

thus they are remarkably effective and we see them again to good effect at Southgate (a shell replacing the semi-circular glazing) and elsewhere later.

The interior of Llanayron is equally attractive and also shares with Southgate Grove a double-return staircase although on a much smaller scale. The double-return staircase, a common enough feature in English 18th-century building, was another feature Nash was to appropriate and use in houses where a round or semi-circular staircase hall was not part

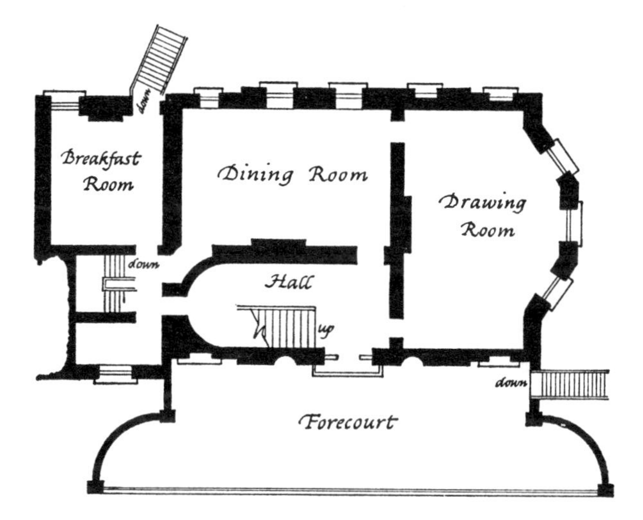

Fig. 6. Foley House, Haverfordwest, *c.* 1794: entrance elevation and ground floor plan.

of the plan. The plan of this house marks the architect's first attempts to juggle about with varied shapes and spatial problems, the dining room having its south wall internally curved and two small upstairs rooms so shaped as to result in a flat elliptical ceiling. Nash was to carry this manipulation, inherited from the Neo-classicism of Adam and Ledoux, several stages further in later Gothic houses.

Foley House, Haverfordwest, was building at the same time as Ffynone and was designed for Richard Foley, a prominent citizen and successful solicitor, whom Nash had met when he was dealing with the restoration of St David's Cathedral.[1] In the small but thriving town of Haverfordwest it must have been quite the most important house. Nash

[1] St David's MSS.

designed it in Palladian style (but with a very English bow projection on the north façade), providing great pediments to all fronts except that connecting the service wing which was, architecturally, supposed not to exist. The north façade is somewhat reminiscent of Ffynone, but the whole villa-like conception with its round-headed windows, pediments and deep eaves takes us on to Southborough Place in Surrey of 1808, and further to 1830, when the small villas in the Park Villages, Regent's Park, were designed. The house first changed hands in 1821 and an advertisement in the *Cambrian* in June of that year described it as '... a capital Modern Mansion House planned by Nash ...'. The character of the building has recently been spoiled by a covering of 'rough-cast'.

A sad relic of another Classical Nash house with the romantic name of Temple Druid lies near Maenclochog, Pembrokeshire. Originally called Bwlch-y-Clawdd, it was re-christened when a nearby cromlech was discovered. It was built for Henry Bulkeley as a medium-sized country seat and was sold in 1821 as '... an excellent mansion house (built by Nash) ...,'[1] but since those days the house has been truncated and reduced to the size and status of a humble farmhouse.

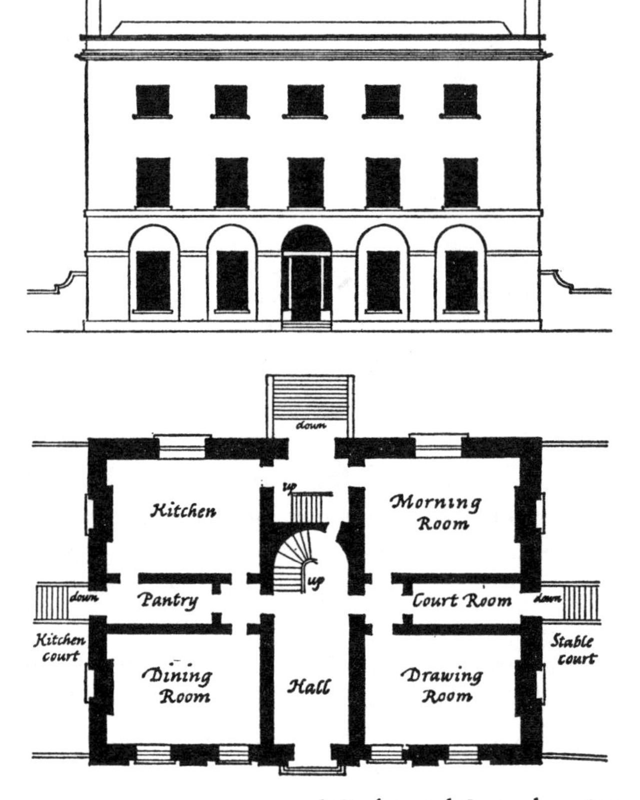

Fig. 7. Whitson Court, Monmouthshire, *c.* 1795: entrance elevation and ground floor plan.

[1] *Cambrian*, 8th September, 1821.

Whitson Court, south-east of Newport, Monmouthshire, represents something quite exceptional in Nash's Classical repertoire. Built of brick in about 1795[1] for William Phillips, it is severely plain and is set in uncompromising moorland. The three-storied central block is flanked by two courts which are enclosed by walls and terminated by balancing wings which resemble pavilions when viewed from the park. The ground-floor windows including those in the wings are set in recessed arches. The square plan is odd in that all the rooms on the ground floor are the same size, the drawing room being no larger than the kitchen; no attempt has been made to use Nash's talent for providing rooms of interesting shape within the confines of a Classical shell. The main staircase is curved with plain balusters and is centrally set at the end of the entrance hall. It is lit by a circular dome above the second floor landing in which is cut a circular opening of the same diameter to light the first floor landing. This opening is provided with a decorative balustrade of small scale to increase the impression of height from below; a sturdier balustrade encircles it out of sight. A service staircase at the rear serves the second floor direct from the ground.

Certain ill-considered additions have spoiled the original severity of the house's appearance, but in the main it survives much as Nash designed it.

After Nash had re-established himself in London he returned to Wales from time to time and Monachty, a plain Palladian house near Llanon, Cardiganshire, should be attributed to him on one of his later visits. It was built for the Rev. Alban Thomas Jones Gwynne, a man of considerable enterprise who was responsible for the replanning of the little nearby river town of Aberayron, an undertaking in which he may have employed the services of Nash.[2] He was also back again to build Aberystwyth Bridge (*c.* 1798), which survived until 1886, but by the time he was building his early Welsh houses, he was already visiting the Isle of Wight and by 1795 he had an office in London. He retained the friendship of many of his Welsh clients and it was through the little group of learned squires at Hafod that he was to meet Humphry Repton, a landscape gardener also immersed in the Picturesque, and with whom he was to work for a while on a much more practical and profitable level.

[1] That the house was designed by Nash is mentioned in Baker's *Guide through Wales*, 1795.

[2] In 1807 Gwynne introduced a Private Bill to Parliament for the development. No evidence can be found to support the theory that Nash laid out the new streets, but the neat terraces of houses contain many features associated with his work.

CHAPTER TWO

The Gothic Ladder

ON 8TH MARCH, 1795, Nash was writing from 30, Duke Street, St James's. He had returned to London with a reputation as an architect of merit filtering from his influential clients in the Welsh countryside, his humble beginnings in Carmarthen (and the long-forgotten disaster in Bloomsbury) well behind him. If the future held its problems Nash was to be equal to them as we shall see; more than that, he almost enjoyed them and if one project failed, he quickly planned something new. His resilience was such that failure aroused challenge; catastrophe stimulated even more challenge. There must have been many occasions when a client would readily have sacked him for one reason or another had not the architect seen to it that the point of no return had been reached. There are instances of clients being on the verge of bankruptcy half-way through a building operation; but Nash was to be responsible for many clients overspending and often his estimates would bear little or no relation to the final cost.[1] For many years he kept anxious clients and angry creditors at bay and until the death of the most illustrious client of all—the King—he manipulated other people's money with a cavalier daring.

Without doubt Nash could have become and remained a country house architect with the most enviable practice in England. There were rivals, notably Soane, Holland, Cockerell, Papworth and James Wyatt; but in their different ways they were poles apart from Nash, not only as architects but also as personalities; and Nash's greatest asset was his thrusting personality. Besides, nobody could be expected to do everything well; Nash certainly didn't, but, more accurately, he did practically everything, whether badly or well. His nature was uncomplicated and uncluttered by profound thinking on any subject. Unlike Soane he was an uninhibited adventurer with an eye to the main chance. He was also the

[1] The building of Caerhayes Castle (*see* p. 41) ruined the owners and in 1852 the whole estate was sold up to meet debts. (County Record Office, Truro.)

5. Casina, Dulwich, *c.* 1797. Repton's landscaping has long since disappeared; from an engraving by J. Hassell for *Views of Noblemen and Gentlemen's Seats, Antiquities and Remarkable Buildings in the Counties adjoining London*, 1804.

6. Southgate Grove, London, *c.* 1797: entrance elevation. Nash's first work in partnership with Humphry Repton; from an Engraving in *New Vitruvius Britannicus*, 1779.

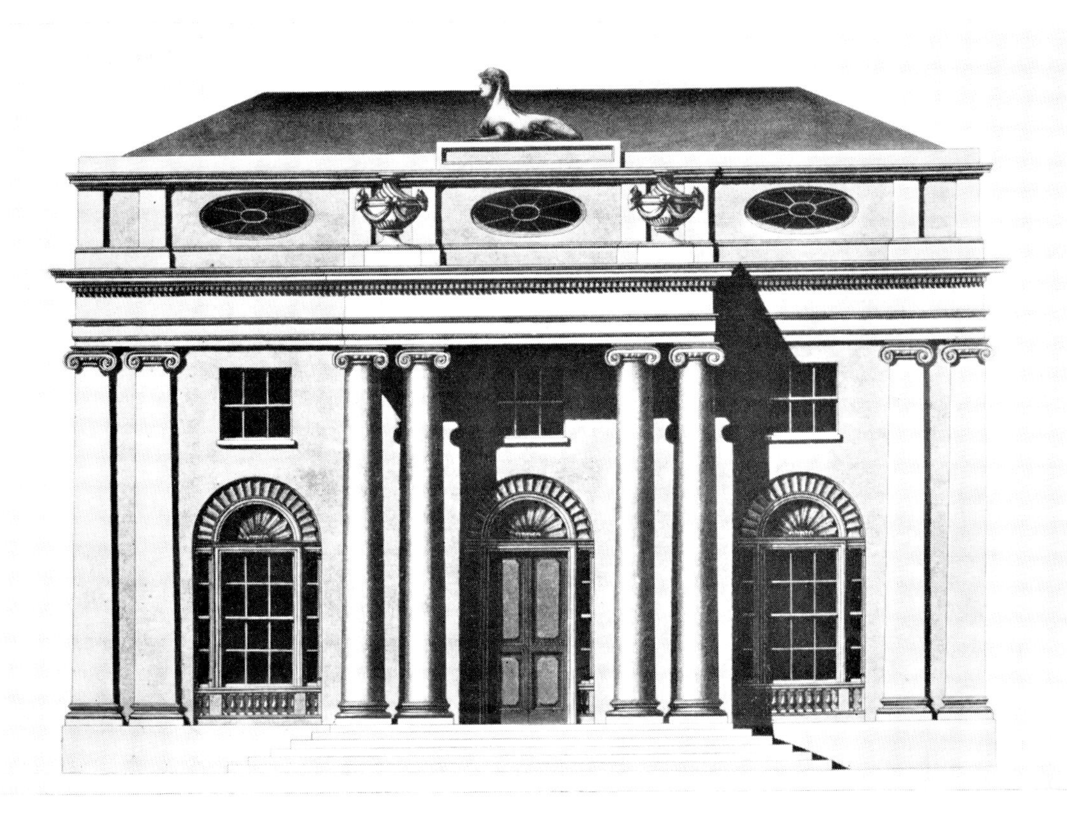

12–16. Blaise Hamlet, Gloucestershire. Five more of the cottages built by Nash for this model village on the outskirts of Bristol. Blaise Hamlet now belongs to the National Trust.

ideal architect for both landed aristocrats with inherited fortunes and the *parvenus.* The former wanted to be in the fashion and many would accept the often pretentious theories of what houses and their surroundings should look like without remotely understanding them; the latter wanted to follow suit and here the scope was unlimited. Nash could satisfy all demands with apparent ease and, busy though he was on his return to London, he was anxious to expand his clientele further and it was not long before his opportunist demands were satisfied.

Humphry Repton was almost exactly the same age as Nash and that was just about all they had in common. In contrast to Nash's brash, jaunty temperament, Repton was quiet, reserved, poetic, sanctimonious; possessing all the qualities, in fact, that Nash lacked. Through friends in his native East Anglia he met the Hafod coterie and shared their serious and intense approach to the related elements in landscape and building, although he was later to quarrel with them.[1]

Repton had seven children, one of whom, John Adey, Nash had recently taken into his Carmarthen office as a draughtsman in 1796. For a time Repton and his family had suffered financial hardship until, in 1788, he was suddenly inspired to turn his passion for landscape gardening into his profession.[2]

By the time Nash had returned to London he was, in a few short years, the unrivalled leader in his chosen career. This, of course, meant that his clients were men of wealth and influence, some of whom not only wanted their land remodelled but also their houses altered or rebuilt in the newly fashionable castle-Gothic style. Although Nash never really understood the style properly, his connection with picturesque, romantic outlines was to become an increasing obsession, whether dealing with a single Gothic house or a street of Classical façades; the seeds of the Picturesque were now deep-rooted and he would apply them for the rest of his life. He was, in a sense, climbing the ladder of success on his slender Gothic gleanings.

For his clients Repton produced his Red Books, many of which survive. They were hand-written and contained his clever water-colour sketches (a talent which he passed on in even greater measure to his son George) showing the client's existing landscape and house and, on lifting a superimposed flap, the suggested alterations—perhaps a new house, a new vista formed by trees, ornamental water and so on. The books were bound in red morocco and were attractive things in themselves. The notes describing the proposals were written in genteel prose, sometimes crystal clear, sometimes meaning very little but always intending to impress. The descriptions conveyed Repton's knowledge and enthusiasm for his subject and at the same time propounded on theories that many clients would have found baffling. In principle he was taking to a further stage his predecessor 'Capability'

[1] *See* Dorothy Stroud: *Humphry Repton*, 1962. The author traces 'the battle of the Picturesque'.
[2] *Ibid*, p. 27.

Brown's desire to provide 'natural' man-made improvements to the scene, making his landscapes softer, subtler and more sympathetic to the character of the land. His proposals for landscaping were couched in such phrases as 'chaste simplicity' and 'apparent extent', just as interior decorators of today talk of 'careful clutter' and 'apparent size' in reference to a room. The aim was to achieve carefully arranged irregularity; nothing obvious; everything vague and suggestive.

We cannot imagine that Nash was over-concerned with the details of these niceties whether they were Repton's or those of Price and Knight. The latter two would continue to theorise for years, quarrel with Repton's views and stick to their own; Nash would learn much from these men and conserve his knowledge for later years when he was laying out parks on a monumental scale; but his only concern at this time was to build.

Repton himself was to design houses in later years, but his enduring enthusiasm was for landscape gardening and he needed someone to provide buildings suited to the theories he was evolving. Nash was the obvious choice; their talents were complementary and a partnership was agreed. Both men knew and admired Downton Castle,[1] Payne Knight's romantic pastiche of 1775—the Classical house disguised as a medieval castle; to both of them, it must have seemed to embody the best of both worlds and the ideal style of building with which to conjure up the complete Picturesque scene.

The commercial basis of the partnership was arranged as follows: Nash was to pay Repton $2\frac{1}{2}\%$ on the cost of any work that came his way through the latter—Nash therefore charged Repton's clients the high fee of 7%, keeping $4\frac{1}{2}\%$ for himself and handing over the balance to Repton.[2] It would be interesting to speculate what the arrangement might have been if Nash had introduced Repton to a client, but there is no record of this having occurred. Nash was on the receiving end and during the partnership he was concerned with over one hundred estates.

The partnership lasted until 1803 and during that time Nash was also occupied with many other projects ranging from a castle he was building for himself in the Isle of Wight to important commissions in Ireland—none of which came through Repton's introduction. The gardens in the Isle of Wight may have been designed by Repton, but otherwise he did not work on any other of Nash's sites outside the partnership.

In spite of their enthusiasm for the castle-Gothic style building in a romantic setting there is little doubt that the partners, perhaps subconsciously, used this formula because it was good business. It was something new to talk about and rich clients were always looking for novelty. When building was required nearly all the estates that Nash and Repton worked on together were provided with a new Gothic house or at least a Gothic face-lift. Sometimes it must have been even better business to forget the whole Gothic idea

[1] *See* Christopher Hussey: *English Country Houses—Mid-Georgian*, 1956.
[2] Farington: *op. cit.*, Vol. I, p. 251.

(especially if the client was a die-hard Palladian) and concentrate on the landscaping. At the end of his career Repton let the whole side down by planting a severely Classical house in the wildest and most haunting coastal scenery[1] and conversely Nash built a Gothic castle, all towers and battlements, in a flat, 'unromantic' and 'unpicturesque' part of Sussex.[2] Nash, of course, was quite prepared to build in any style as long as he was working and during the partnership his houses were Classical, Gothic, 'Tudor' or hybrids of all three.

The first time we hear of the partners working together is at Southgate Grove in north London where, in 1797, Nash built his first large Classical mansion and possibly his best. In 1797 Southgate was an attractive village conveniently near London, later to be swallowed up by 19th- and 20th-century suburban sprawl. The client was Mr Walker Gray and Repton landscaped the grounds beautifully. With its urns, sphinxes and oval attic windows the house has a faintly French air.[3] We shall see these elements again elsewhere, but here they are used with assurance and a scholarly appreciation of their values. Although Southgate appears grander than it really is, the almost square plan (a legacy from Wales) is compact and none of the rooms is grandiose. The main ground floor rooms, which can be opened up to form one large space, are subordinated to a spacious, central, double-return staircase, approached by a stone-flagged entrance hall with a vaulted plaster ceiling containing a circular panel of radial fluting; and there are delicately executed grisaille paintings over each door.[4] The building survives and is used as a convalescent home; the grounds, now a public park, have lost their former luxuriance, but still add a welcome note of greenery to this now drab part of the London scene.

For their next joint undertaking Nash designed a most original house at Dulwich and one which combined elements used in several later works. It was called Casina and was also built in the busy year of 1797 for Richard Shawe, solicitor to Warren Hastings whose patronage provided him with a fair fortune. J. Dallaway in his *Anecdotes of the Arts in England* (1800) described the house as '. . . a new style of Country House . . . combining the advantages of an English arrangement with the beauty of a Palladian plan'. Certainly it was novel and no doubt attracted a good deal of attention at the time. The garden front consisted of a curved domed pavilion (containing a circular room) flanked by two Ionic wings of single-storey height with a vast square window in each flanked by round-headed niches and surmounted by a balustrade. The elevation did not look unlike an orangery, but this pleasing effect was spoiled, for behind was attached a large rectangular block containing the real house ('the English arrangement') which rose to the height of the dome, displaying

[1] Sheringham Hall, Norfolk. [2] Knepp Castle, Sussex (*see* p. 40).

[3] There are fine engravings of both main elevations in G. Richardson, *New Vitruvius Britannicus*, 1799. Repton made a small water-colour drawing of the house and park for Peacock's Polite Repository, 1798, now at the British Museum.

[4] *See* illustrations of the entrance hall and staircase in Davis: *op. cit.*

a blank wall to the garden. Nevertheless it was an intriguing building with much charm. It was demolished in 1906.

1797 was also the year in which Repton introduced Nash to work at Corsham Court, the Wiltshire seat of P. C. Methuen. Nash had apparently visited Corsham as early as 1793—the time when he was starting to venture from his Welsh commitments—but he did not work there until after Repton had been called in to improve the park. It is here that we see the first instance of Nash ousting an architect already on the scene, James Wyatt, who had earlier been consulted by Methuen. Nash may have given one of his optimistic estimates, unfavourable to Wyatt, or the client may have been impressed with the idea of two people working together on the same scheme; we do not know.[1] The extensive alterations and additions to the house were all in elaborate Tudor-Gothic style, a projection on the north front flanked by twin cupolas was derived from Henry VII's Chapel at Westminster and may have been designed by J. A. Repton.[2] The house was largely remodelled by Bellamy in the mid-19th century and most of Nash's work, except the library, disappeared.

Sundridge Park near Bromley in Kent was another, but larger, Classical house again with a circular central pavilion and flanking wings but designed as a single block.[3] It seems that here again Wyatt was dropped after the owner, a Mr Linde, sold the estate to Mr Claude Scott in 1796, and Nash stepped in. There are suggestions here that Repton had his first quarrel with Nash over the design of the house, though when he said he regretted 'having shared with another the reputation of designing and adapting this very singular house to circumstances which cannot well be explained but upon the spot . . .'[4], he might have been referring to the problem of using Wyatt's original plan which Nash probably adapted. It would have been early in the partnership to have crossed swords with Nash. The house is now used as a country hotel; Repton's grounds are used as a golf-course and the house was 'Adamised'—to no good effect—at a later date.

It would not be possible here to trace the pair over all the works on which they collaborated, but before we progress to more of Nash's own works there are certain houses produced by the partnership which we should examine. One of these is Luscombe Castle (1800) near Dawlish, Devon, and is interesting because it represents the nearest the two came to the Picturesque ideal.[5] It has faults, is not a very successful piece of planning, and had to be altered within a short while after completion. An ancillary Gothic bay was added to the tower containing the octagonal drawing room, thereby spoiling the latter's

[1] *See* Stroud: *op. cit.*, p. 95.

[2] *Ibid*: the north front is illustrated.

[3] There is a view of the house in W. Angus: *Seats of the Nobility and Gentry*, 1797.

[4] J. C. Loudon: *The Landscape Gardening and the Landscape Architecture of the late Humphry Repton Esq.*, 1840.

[5] A description of the house is given by Christopher Hussey, *Country Life*, February 9th, 1956. *See* also N. Pevsner: *The Buildings of England*; *S. Devon*, 1952, and Christopher Hussey: *English Country Houses*; *Late Georgian*, 1958.

shape and confusing an otherwise compact, castellated garden front. The general appearance was more 'Tudor' than Gothic, an effect Nash was to give to East Cowes Castle, Caerhayes in Cornwall and Lough Cutra in Galway. A Gothic bay added here or there was of no account and was thought to add to the overall picturesque effect; one of the advantages of the Gothic style, as the Picturesque theory made clear, was that exteriors could be juggled round convenient plans instead of the reverse where plans had to be fitted, often inconveniently, behind Classical façades. More often than not seemingly frivolous towers or turrets fulfilled important roles in the planning; they provided otherwise dull rooms with bays and apses and sometimes contained circular staircases and rooms. In spite of Gothic and Tudor windows the interior of Luscombe has Classical decoration—yet another aspect of the Theory's flexibility. It was built for the Hoare family, the bankers, in whose possession it remains today.[1]

By now Nash was achieving a formidable reputation as an architect specialising in the neo-medieval Castle style and, profiting from his work with Repton, had fully identified himself with the Gothic taste. He had built several large Gothic castles on his own account and scattered picturesque cottages, lodges and stabling over the great estates of his clients in the West Country and elsewhere.

These attractive small buildings have never been fully recorded and would form the basis of a long and rewarding thesis. The most celebrated group of cottages designed by Nash are at Blaise, Somerset.[2] He had already designed a conservatory[3] at Blaise Castle for J. S. Harford at the end of the Repton partnership in 1803 and he was recalled in 1811 to build Blaise Hamlet, a series of rustic cottages set round a green, complete with village pump (incorporating a sundial) and many other 'countryfied' touches to establish the Picturesque ideal. That Nash took cottage design seriously is borne out by his letter to Mrs Stewart of Killymoon of 1805.[4] These charming cottages and the later groups in the Park Villages, Regents Park, were to degenerate into Victorian villas of a more ponderous kind and, worse, to be the forerunners of 'picturesque' suburbia at the hands of ignorant builders of the 20th century.

About this time Nash was also working nearby at Barnsley Park in Gloucestershire. Between 1806 and 1810 he designed the elegant library, an Ionic conservatory (similar to the ones he was later to build at Buckingham Palace) and an entrance lodge.[5] Nash's

[1] Stonelands, a plain Classical house existing nearby, also built by the Hoare family *c.* 1817, may be attributed to Nash.

[2] Original drawings for each cottage are in one of George Repton's note-books at the Royal Pavilion, Brighton.

[3] A Druidical folly had also been proposed. *See* drawing in another of George Repton's notebooks, Royal Institute of British Architects.

[4] *See* p. 49.

[5] See *Country Life*, Vol. CXVI, p. 723. A design for another cottage is in George Repton's notebook (Royal Pavilion). *See* also design for a lodge. Documents concerning Nash's work here are at the Bodleian Library, Oxford. (MS.D.D. Wykeham Musgrave, *c.* 22).

English Empire decorations for the library perfectly express the shape of the great bay window of the original house.

A house in the Blaise vein was a whimsical villa near Liphook, Hampshire, of *c.* 1800. Drawings[1] show it to include all the most desired features in the *cottage ornée* style—thatched roof and thatched projecting bays, crenellated bargeboarding and small windows incorporating Classical and Gothic elements; a latticed porch was surmounted by a dome hinting at the Oriental. The house was rebuilt in the 1890s. This gradual absorption with the cottage style culminated in his design for a vast thatched 'cottage' for George IV in 1812–14.

Fig. 8. Longner Hall, Shropshire, 1806. A stone-built house in Tudor style with an elaborate Gothic interior; from George Repton's Notebook (R.I.B.A.).

However, until 1803 Nash was still involved with Repton whose fourth son, George Stanley, had joined Nash's office about 1795. George Stanley Repton remained in the office even after the break-up of the partnership, became an excellent draughtsman and eventually chief assistant until he set up on his own as an architect in 1820. His notebooks of meticulous drawings and sketches throw interesting light on the work being done in Nash's office at the time and confirm that he and his staff were prolific purveyors of the Gothic taste.

During these busy years Nash was often an absentee partner and because of his inability to concentrate on any one project long enough to do it justice (there are many instances of clients wondering if their houses would ever be finished), his work varied in interest and quality to an alarming degree. Not only was he visiting his insular sites—as far north as Scotland[2] and south to Cornwall—but he was also working in Ireland. He told Farington

[1] In George Repton's notebook. (R.I.B.A.). Now called 'Hollycombe'.

[2] In December, 1796, Nash wrote to Philipps of Cwmgwli: 'Just returned from ye cursedest journey to Scotland I have ever experienced.' This was probably in connection with work for Lord Selkirk at Kirkcudbright. There is a design for a cottage in George Repton's notebook (R.I.B.A.).

that he had 'travelled in the Three Kingdoms eleven thousand miles in the year and in that time he had expended £1,500 in chaise hire'. Even today some of the sites are remote and difficult to get to and we cannot but admire the enormous physical energy and determination required to travel under conditions which in those days would have been disagreeable in the extreme.

The last time we hear of Nash and Repton co-operating was over an estate in Shropshire, a county where Nash had done other work close by. It is a curious house called Longner Hall built for Robert Burton in about 1806. But the co-operation must have been stormy as by then the partnership had terminated in bitterness. Nash, in Repton's eyes, had not sufficiently appreciated the talents of his son John Adey, who therefore left the former's office and joined his father; also Repton could see that, once established through his introductions, Nash would stop at nothing to advance himself, and when royal patronage was on the horizon he would grab it for himself.

At Longner the client somehow employed them at the same time and a stone 'Tudor' house emerged. The drawing of it in George Repton's Notebook[1] shows an open verandah with Gothic arches and a conservatory in similar style to the left, but it appears that this was abandoned in favour of glazing the verandah and omitting the conservatory—although not an addition *per se*, a similar story to that of Luscombe. The interior is entirely Gothic with elaborate plaster fan-vaulting in the main rooms and a staircase hall where the undercarriage of the first floor landing terminates in free-standing pendents.[2]

To illustrate the uneven quality of Nash's work we should look briefly at his other Gothic houses in England. Apart from his own castle at East Cowes to which we shall return later, there were six others of considerable size. The two least interesting (and both demolished) are Childwall Hall in Lancashire and Garnstone[3] in Herefordshire. Besides sharing the same fate, and both being built in 1806, they had many architectural elements in common—the asymmetrical grouping of towers and buttresses to give a picturesque effect—and give the impression that the addition of another tower or so would neither enhance nor spoil the compositions. This is not so with Nash's better compositions such as West Grinstead Park, Sussex (*c.* 1806 and fallen into decay) where, although the outline is still irregular and picturesque, the grouping of the main elements is compact and 'complete'. At West Grinstead the main features of the Gothic interior were a double-return staircase[4] and a circular dining room. The latter contained a Gothic cornice, the ribs of which were extended to form fluted wall panels. The house was greatly enlarged in the 1860s.

[1] At the R.I.B.A.

[2] *See* illustrations of the interior in Davis: *op. cit. See* also Pevsner: *op. cit.*, *Shropshire*, 1958.

[3] Nash's building replaced an interesting 17th-century brick house with open forecourt and bayed porch. *See* C. J. Robinson: *The Mansions of Herefordshire and Their Memories*, 1873.

[4] *See* illustration of staircase in Davis: *op. cit.* There is a plan in George Repton's notebook (R.I.B.A.). *See* also Nairn and Pevsner: *op. cit.*, *Sussex*, 1965.

Close to West Grinstead lies Knepp Castle built in 1809–12 for Sir Charles Burrell, Father of the House of Commons, and brother of Walter Burrell of West Grinstead Park. The name 'Knepp' was taken from the Norman ruin which stands on a small prominent hill a mile away.

It is set in the flat country of the Sussex Weald overlooking a fifty-acre lake and is only fifty feet above sea level. It is a good example of a moderate-sized country house disguised

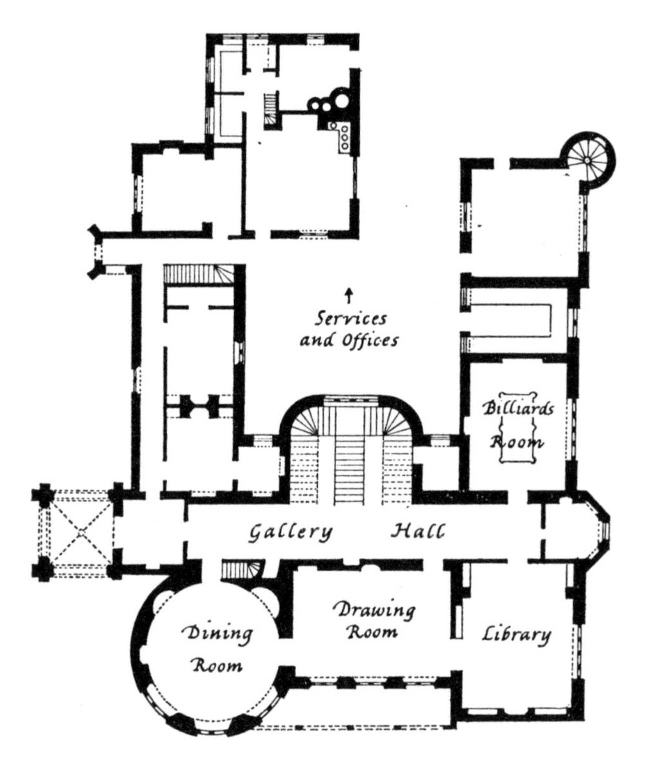

Fig. 9. West Grinstead Park, Sussex: ground floor plan (*See* Plate 21).

as a castle. A round tower contains an elegant circular stone cantilevered staircase with a circular bedroom above it and all the interior details are Gothic. To the north-west the large stable courtyard buildings were, like the chimneys of the house, left in unrendered red brick, presumably because money ran out before completion. The main body of the house is cement-rendered and incised to imitate stone blocks. A view from the roof, however, reveals how vain was this deceit as the red brick portions appear infinitely more medieval than Nash's cement. The builder was Alexander Kyffin and all the bricks were baked on site and the timber gathered from the estate. We are told that the client 'consulted Mr Nash, an Architect of eminence, who furnished him with a plan for the building,'[1] and that the cost was £28,500 of which £9,500 was for decorations. In 1904 a severe fire

[1] Burrell Estate Papers.

gutted the main part of the house which was subsequently reinstated and somewhat altered.

Ravensworth Castle in County Durham was the most ambitious Gothic house and perhaps the worst of all. It was built in 1808 for a prominent industrialist, Sir Thomas Liddell, Bart, later Lord Ravensworth and friend of the Prince Regent, and, including two ancient towers that were retained in the composition, no fewer than twelve towers and turrets can be counted in a contemporary engraving.[1] The Gothic detail, however, was of good quality and may have been supplied by Pugin who was now working in the London office and who published *Specimens of Gothic Architecture* ... at this time. The house was much altered in the mid-19th century and was demolished in 1953. In the original drawings,[2] the plans show more skill and ingenuity than the elevations.

Caerhayes Castle built for J. Trevanion in 1808 is one of Nash's more successful Gothic designs and commands magnificent views of the Cornish coast and surrounding countryside. Here we see once more the round and square blocks and the turrets used to make a satisfying composition while still retaining the Romantic ideal, unlike the unfortunate Garnstone which managed to be both rambling and dull. The interior is a naïve and charming mixture of Classical and Gothic decoration. The long vaulted hall, top-lit by a galleried opening, leads to an imposing double-return staircase hall set beyond a broad arch supported on scroll corbels. A stable courtyard and other outbuildings are later additions, but otherwise the house remains much as when built.

The last Gothic house in the English group that we must consider is Aqualate Hall, Staffordshire, enlarged in the same year for Sir J. F. Boughey, Bart. Although only partial (but substantial) additions to an earlier house, the design possessed some of those touches of fantasy that make the architect such an absorbing subject of study. The characteristics that set it well apart from the other Gothic houses were buttresses at the corners of castellated octagonal bays extending into pinnacles forming a crown around well-shaped ogee domes. Remove these frills and we are left with a composition something like one of Nash's duller Gothic houses. He had built nothing quite like this before[3] and it was his only stuccoed Gothic mansion. Aqualate took its attractive name from the Mere, a natural stretch of water nearby. It replaced a 17th-century house which in turn had replaced the ancient Hall of Aquylot. All Nash's work was destroyed in a fire of 1910.[4]

So far the development of Nash's tastes and styles are easily followed. The Welsh

[1] *See* T. Rowe: *Westmorland, Cumberland, Durham & Northumberland*, 1832.

[2] At the R.I.B.A. *See* also Pevsner: *op. cit.*, Co. Durham, 1953.

[3] Nash had proposed similar ogival domes in a Gothic design for Magdalen College, Oxford, in 1801 (not executed) and used them at St Mary's Church, Haggerston, 1826 (destroyed by bombs, 1940). Domed bays appear in a proposal for rebuilding Carlton House (*see* p. 94) and in Sussex Place, Regent's Park (*see* p. 68). Nash's inspiration may have been similar elements at Houghton and Wrotham.

[4] There is a plan in George Repton's notebook (Royal Pavilion).

houses represent the practical result of his late-Palladian training with Taylor; the Gothic houses follow on from his first thoughts about the style at St David's and with the Hafod group and expressed in his work with Repton. He had emerged therefore as one of the last of the Classicists and one of the first of the Gothicists, combining elements of both styles in realising the Picturesque. But there is another style which, although derivative, he made entirely his own—the Italianate Villa style. It is sad that only three houses of this very agreeable type are known to exist; they have a strange attraction.

We see the same square and round towers, but here they present smooth stuccoed elevations pierced by rectangular or round-headed sash windows and with deeply overhanging eaves. In two of the examples the main blocks are linked by open colonnades. Here was the perfect country villa that was neither Gothic nor Classical but still possessed the romantic outline of the former and the simplicity of the latter.

Nash's original inspiration for his Italianate villas is obscure,[1] but houses with round towers and conical roofs were often seen in northern Italy and in the romantic landscapes of Claude, Boucher and other continental painters; or perhaps Hamstead, an old house he bought near East Cowes at about this time, served as a starting point. There he made a feature of an ancient round tower when remodelling the building and may have thought the idea worth developing. He topped the tower with a conical thatched roof.[2]

The earliest and most important villa is Cronkhill, near Shrewsbury, built in 1802 for the agent of Lord Berwick of nearby Attingham Park in 1802; no doubt plans to build a house were discussed when Nash was working at Attingham in 1798. Later Nash returned to design the picture gallery and staircase for Lord Berwick.[3]

We have seen the broad, overhanging eaves and round-headed windows in Wales and Nash was to use them again at another country house, Southborough Place,[4] Surrey, but in a rectangular Palladian design. At Cronkhill these features take on an altogether different character, used here with curved and flat surfaces and on different planes. The stone arcaded verandah links the three main blocks and the service wing is hidden by shrubbery. The house is finely set on a well-wooded hill facing the distant Wrekin; but it would be easy to imagine this house enhancing any surroundings.[5]

On the eastern bank of the Dart, high against a once well-timbered background, stands another impressive Italianate villa, Sandridge Park, near Dartmouth. It was built in 1805 for the widow of the first Lord Ashburton and commands views of the greatest beauty. The

[1] Professor Pevsner suggests the influence of the Southern farmhouse. See *An Outline of European Architecture* (6th Ed.), 1960, p. 622.

[2] There is a drawing in George Repton's notebook (R.I.B.A.).

[3] *c.* 1810. There is a drawing of the gallery at Attingham. *See* also Pevsner: *op. cit.*, Shropshire.

[4] *See* illustrations of the exterior in Davis: *op. cit.*

[5] A pale reflection of the Italianate villas is Wood Hall, Skirlaugh, Yorkshire, by Charles Mountain, *c.* 1820. A round tower is combined with Palladian elements in a severe unrendered brick composition.

house was neglected and the estate shorn of most of its fine timber in recent years, but happily the house has been restored by a recent owner, the Earl Cathcart. As at Cronkhill, the round and square towers are there, but the arrangement is reversed. The round tower is dominated by the other blocks and there is no colonnade to link the elements. Originally a trellised Oriental-style conservatory to the right of the front door was the first feature to be enjoyed when approaching the house,[1] but this has vanished as has the ironwork to the central balcony.

Cronkhill's colonnade was a clever linking device, but Sandridge's conservatory was no such thing—merely an attractive and fashionable requirement of the day which Nash and others supplied to order. Thus Sandridge must take second place to Cronkhill as a piece of design. The elements, although they make a pleasing group, are less thoughtfully disposed, the composition is less successful and the impact we feel at Cronkhill is missing.

The interior of Sandridge is very severe indeed and all the details are in restrained Classical vein. As at West Grinstead, the round tower contains a circular dining room (one of the few towers to contain an important circular room), and the first floor corridor, approached by a surprisingly plain staircase with wood balusters, is pleasantly vaulted somewhat in the manner of Soane and lit by a circular dome.[2]

The third Italianate villa lies some forty miles due west of Belfast; but Nash's Irish works merit a chapter to themselves.

[1] There is a design for a circular conservatory in the same style in George Repton's notebook (Royal Pavilion).

[2] *See* illustrations of the staircase and landing in Davis: *op. cit.*

CHAPTER THREE

Island Demesnes

AT the turn of the century fashionable Dublin was a Georgian city with good reason to be proud of its streets and squares. Those who had country estates visited their town houses when it suited them; those with commercial pursuits lived in them all the time. There was never to be any sign of change in the endless rows of brick façades; no rendering with plaster to be in line with modish trends from London; nor was the greenery of Phoenix Park to be fringed with terraces of stuccoed mansions and dotted with Classical villas. Had this happened, a visitor to Ireland in the 1820s might well have thought he was in England, for in the countryside had sprung up certain new houses—some vaguely familiar—and all designed by Nash.

Although the Irish houses span dates that overlap Nash's work elsewhere they represent a remarkably complete picture of his domestic architecture from the time of his return to London until he gave up country house building to become a servant of the Crown. They are therefore worth considering together, as were the Welsh houses, but for different reasons. The latter were pointers to the future, the others form a précis of his English works. They are also the least explored of his works and for that reason alone make a rewarding study.

Documentation on the houses is, unfortunately, extremely rare and until recently it was almost entirely of English origin, but newly discovered letters relating to Killymoon Castle[1] help to build up a stronger picture of Nash's activities than has hitherto been possible.

A letter from Lord Lorton,[2] for whom Nash built a house, to Colonel Stewart of

[1] Here called 'The Clements Papers', most of the correspondence is in the possession of Mr Marcus Clements, of Lough Rynn, Co. Leitrim, descendant of the builder of Killymoon. Certain of the letters, however, are in the National Library of Ireland (MSS Dept., Murray Coll. PF. 27)

[2] *See* extract from letter, p. 53.

Killymoon states that Nash had been to see him in 1809 and represents the only first-hand record we have that Nash visited a particular site in person though proposals for visits are mentioned in other letters. It is unlikely at this stage that Nash would miss the opportunity of being in close touch with such influential clients, but in later years when he was busy in London he sent drawings over and left the supervision of building to others.

A drawing of Killymoon was exhibited in the Royal Academy of 1803, but the house can be given an earlier date as the Earl of Selkirk, for whom Nash worked in Scotland,[1] wrote to the owner from Inverness in 1802: 'I am happy to hear so good accounts of your Castle: I hope it will be an introduction to a good taste of Architecture in your quarter of the Kingdom....'

A little to the west of the long, wide, main street of Cookstown, Co. Tyrone, the country suddenly changes into undulating parkland, heralded by a 'Tudor' archway with lodge—the remains of the Killymoon demesne. But a nostalgic description, given in the details of the sale of the property in the 1880s, helps one to arrive at the castle on a happier note and to appreciate what life must have been like on a moderate-sized Irish country estate:[2]

> ... The Killymoon Demesne, situated in one of the best districts in Ireland, and widely celebrated for its picturesque beauty, contains 585 acres of excellent well drained, arable and pasture land, and is almost entirely surrounded by a well-built wall from 10 to 12 feet high.
>
> The ground of the Park is beautifully undulated, interspersed with plantations, and studded throughout with clumps of forest trees, and timber of splendid growth, and is intersected for the entire length by two rivers which unite near the Mansion House. The Park is entered by four Lodges and avenues at different points, and contains two valuable Stone Quarries, a Lime Quarry and Kiln, a Gravel Pit, also a few acres of Bog Turf, and is provided with Laborers' Cottages and two Ornamental Cottages.
>
> The Mansion House (for many generations the seat of the Stewart family) is of dressed stone, in the castellated style, and was built by the well-known architect of Carlton House, Joseph Nash,[3] and is in good repair. It stands upon rising ground, which forms a natural terrace, at a short distance from the junction of the two rivers, the views of which it commands, and is in every way a suitable residence for a nobleman or gentleman of fortune, no expense having been spared in the decorations, fittings and appointments.... The walled Flower and Kitchen Gardens, with Lawns and Ornamental Shrubberies, are laid out with the greatest taste, and comprise about twelve acres (exclusive of several miles of picturesque walks through the park and woods) and

[1] *See* footnote: p. 38.
[2] The Clements Papers, N.L.I.
[3] Here confused with the 19th-century artist (1808–78).

> are furnished with a great variety of flowers and shrubs, and contain extensive vineries, peach, and fig houses in full bearing, conservatory, stove, mushroom and forcing houses, potting sheds, tool houses, two excellent gardeners' dwelling houses, ice house, etc. The walls are covered with every kind of choice fruit trees in good bearing. . . . The Rivers, which are strictly preserved, abound in trout, and the fishing is excellent. The covers are well stocked with pheasants, and there is an abundance of wild fowl; woodcocks are extremely numerous in the season, most of the underwood in the covers being laurel.

As if this description might fail to attract a purchaser, Sir Joseph Paxton, the distinguished landscape designer and engineer, added the following testimonial: 'I have visited most of the celebrated country seats in the United Kingdom, and a very large number on the Continent, and I have never seen one (for the extent of it) more compact, more perfect, in itself, than Killymoon, where the highest natural beauties have been more aided by refined taste and Judgement.' It seems that Lord Selkirk's hopes of 1802 had been fulfilled.

Although it has cousins in England (West Grinstead is the nearest relation) Killymoon is certainly a remarkable house and possesses many original features—some of them untutored and naïve but adding up to a very attractive whole. Some of Nash's later houses

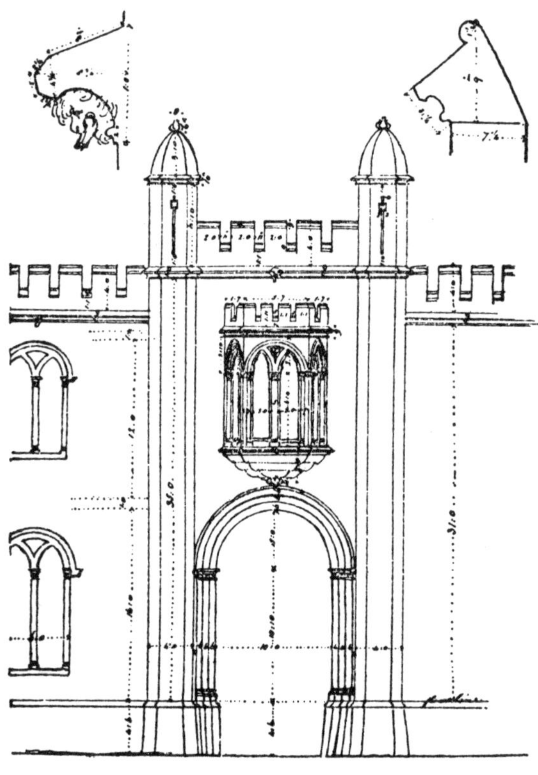

Fig. 10. Killymoon Castle: the massive *porte-cochère* on the entrance elevation (*See* Plate 27); from George Repton's Notebook (R.I.B.A.).

are spectacular but not captivating; Killymoon is both. Like Hafod, it is a house to dream about. Photographs of the exterior do not do it justice—especially as the house now has several important details missing—and the drawing of the south front in George Repton's Notebook[1] must serve as the ideal vision and its near realisation. Here the towers and the great *porte-cochère* make a varied but integrated composition in Saxon Gothic vein and perhaps the house would have been a good deal duller had Nash's detailing of windows and the fenestration in general been more scholarly and orderly. But the thing one notices at once is the high quality of the materials and workmanship employed. The stone is cut very finely and the window tracery is of solid oak; only when we discover that some of the battlements are also made of oak does a deceitful note creep in.

The main feature of the interior is the staircase approached by a narrow flight of steps in a highly vaulted entrance corridor, through a rectangular inner hall and finally into the great staircase hall. It is a considerable progress and the effect is dramatic. The double-return staircase with Gothic balusters (identical to those at West Grinstead and Longner) rises to a first floor gallery lit by a Gothic clerestory below an immense lantern edged with purple glass. This in turn is supported on vaulted arches ending in pendants. The staircase hall gives on to the ante-room linking drawing room and dining room on the garden front and, behind the staircase itself, the library and study. The inner hall, also, gives access to the dining room and a square room with columned annexe, presumably the morning room, to the east. The least satisfactory of this series of attractive rooms is the drawing room with its deeply coved cornices filled with wreaths and honeysuckle, its six-light Saxon window in the south wall and the fitted round-topped pier-glasses in the chamfered corners. It seems that Mrs Stewart too was daunted by this room for she wrote to Nash asking how she could curtain the windows. His reply shows him not above taking trouble with such details and after some delay he writes:[2]

> Madam, Mrs Nash will have informed you that I have been constantly travelling for 2 months past and consequently have never had the power of answering your questions respecting curtains etc. etc. There are a variety of forms which may be adapted to the windows at Killymoon notwithstanding there may not be more than an inch between the moulding of the Window and bottom of the Cornice—for ye present I send 2 slight sketches merely to show you how they may be formed—in the one a circular brass rod of $\frac{3}{4}$ of an Inch diameter resting on 2 pateras (or heads or masks) of the exact sweep of the windows is fixed 3 Inches or 2 Inches from the wall from which or round which drapery may be formed either visibly turning over the rod or concealed underneath a vandyke or other enriched border as shown in the sketch or under a hollow cornice—the whole of which may be looped up to the form in the drawing or any other form

[1] R.I.B.A. [2] The Clements Papers, N.L.I.

> or the head drapery may be fixed and the underdrapery only looped up—the other sketch is to shew how the head may be made straight—in which case should be an inch diameter finished at each end as a thyrsus or with any other termination—this rod is also fixed about three inches from the wall and the drapery may fold over as in the sketch. . . .

and so on for another page. Poor Mrs Stewart who, in her letters, does not appear a very stalwart woman when faced with problems, must have realised that Nash had left the field wide open and in spite of his sketches and instructions had to make up her own mind after all. But, baffled again, she was later writing to Mrs Nash for help with the wretched curtains.

The dining room, an extension of the round tower, is the most successful. Although oval in plan, the room is sub-divided by the inclusion of an apse with a lower ceiling height at the north end. Great effect is obtained by the skilful use of plain ceiling beds combined with fluted spandrels and other mouldings carrying the eye towards the higher part of the room with its cornice of deeply carved paterae. This was spatial harmony in the Soane manner and used with much ingenuity.

Alas, all did not run smoothly with the building of Killymoon. Colonel William Stewart was an absentee client and much of the brunt of supervision fell into the frail hands of his wife. He appears to have been a much adulated local squire whose family had held property in Cookstown since 1634, and a contemporary ballad runs thus:

A NEW SONG IN PRAISE OF COLONEL STEWART

Ye bards of Erin O pray excuse me,
These simple lines for to lay down.
It is concerning a worthy Landlord,
That lives convenient unto Cookstown.
His worthy talents deserve great Honour,
His principles being both firm and pure,
He is a friend and credit to his tenants round him,
And a benefactor to all the poor.

A simple song indeed, but he was apparently a popular squire and much bound up in local affairs notably in yeomanry and church matters. There is, however, another side to things and while he was representing his constituency in Parliament, leaving his wife behind for long stretches at a time, he was involved with the Prince Regent's racy set at Carlton House. Here, it is said, Stewart 'lost' Killymoon in a night's gambling (a high stake by any standards as the house is said to have cost £80,000), but that the next day the Prince

17. Barnsley Park, Gloucestershire, *c.* 1810, the library: a room remodelled and decorated in Empire style.

18. Liphook, Hampshire, *c.* 1800: a villa in *cottage-ornée* style which Nash developed and modified at Blaise, Windsor, the Park Villages and on many country estates; from George Repton's Notebook (R.I.B.A.).

19. Childwall Hall, Lancashire, 1806: one of Nash's least successful exercises in Gothic; engraved from a drawing by J. P. Neale for *Views of the Seats of Noblemen and Gentlemen in England, Wales, Scotland and Ireland*, 2nd series, Vol II, 1824–29.

20. Garnstone, Herefordshire, *c.* 1806: a rambling building lacking the compactness of Nash's better irregular Gothic compositions; engraved from a drawing by Neale for *Views of the Seats of Noblemen and Gentlemen in England, Wales, Scotland and Ireland.*

21. West Park Grinstead, Sussex, *c.* 1806: a brilliant plan was here well combined with the ideal romantic exterior; from George Repton's Notebook (R.I.B.A.).

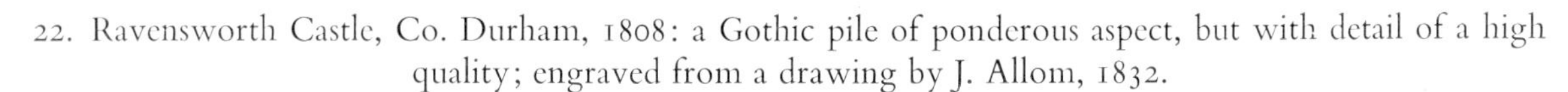

22. Ravensworth Castle, Co. Durham, 1808: a Gothic pile of ponderous aspect, but with detail of a high quality; engraved from a drawing by J. Allom, 1832.

23. Caerhayes Castle, Cornwall, 1808: belonging to the group of successful castle-Gothic houses.

24. Aqualate Hall, Staffordshire, 1808: the Gothic additions show Nash's first use of ogee domes which he also proposed for a rebuilding of Carlton House and for Magdalen College, Oxford. The bays and domes were later used in modified form in Sussex Place, Regent's Park; engraved from a drawing by S. Bourne, 1825; the William Salt Library, Stafford.

sent him a scornful note telling him to 'keep his Irish cabin'[1]—a poor tribute to Nash and to Mrs Stewart who was left struggling with the builders. Her letters are full of despair at her husband's constant absences: '. . . in your absence my happiest moments are those I dedicate to you . . .'; 'every day I grow so tired of being without you . . .'; '. . . my fortitude diminishes shockingly . . .'. But more important to our story are her remarks concerning the building of the house. During this time the Stewarts also had a house in Dublin and Mrs Stewart spent a good deal of her time packing bags and children into the coach between Dublin and Cookstown. No wonder she was tired of being without her husband for in 1805 things were still being built at Killymoon and among her other responsibilities she had to interpret the following letter from Nash:[2]

Dover Street,
April 10 1805

Madam,

I have taken the liberty to draw out your cottage in detail for the workmen—it is a very good plan and will make a very pretty cottage. The cutboard up the gables was not originally intended as ornament, but merely to cover the ends of the timbers beyond the walls and if you use them for the same purpose the effect will be good because the purpose will be rational therefore you must desire Bevans[3] to let the ridge piece, the two purlins and the wall plates project beyond the wall about 6 inches and nail the bargeboards against the ends of those timbers so projecting—this notch board is generally accompanied with a piece of wood shaped like a pinnacle at the point where they meet—I have drawn the board and the pinnacle to a quarter of its real size—the Gothic labels over the windows do not belong to the character of the cottage unless they are gothic Cottages—which is an affected stile of Cottage and I think your good taste will reject. I therefore recommend in lieu of the gothic labels a penthouse board from 6 to 9 inches broad supported by 2 or 3 brackets over the windows to carry off the water and to take from the flat appearance of the window—the kitchen window I apprehend you mean should project—which will have a good effect—but the ends projecting should be glazed which I presume you intend if the glass at the ends are 9 inches wide it will be sufficient—I have taken the liberty to enclose designs of another Cottage made on the same plan as your own—thinking you might wish to build another and would prefer some variety.

Mr Stewart has communicated to me your difficulty in getting Bevans to understand

[1] Information of Robin Bryans, author of *Ulster, a Journey through the Six Counties*, 1964.

[2] The Clements Papers, N.L.I.

[3] Stewart's builder.

your meaning about the bargeboards—I hope I shall be more successful with him. I beg my respects to the Miss Stewarts and your sons—I have the honour to be Madam,

Yr most faithful & Obedient Servant
John Nash

Mrs Stewart was therefore involved with everything from drawing room curtains to cottage bargeboards, but the letter also reveals a little of Nash's character and his method of dealing with clients. No doubt he and Stewart met in London to discuss the plans, the latter begging the architect to send something to occupy his wife while he was away. This Nash did, blending a fairly subtle mixture of flattery with detailed information; the letter also shows Nash's innate tendency to suggest a new idea (in this case a second cottage) before the first one was finished. Later in his career this was to apply to whole planning schemes in London and elsewhere, sometimes with chaotic results.

As Killymoon is, at present, the only Irish house with documents throwing light on its architect and its building, it is worth recording two more extracts from Mrs Stewart's letters. In one, undated, but probably fairly early on in the building, she writes to her husband:[1] '... I forgot one thing last post which was to assure you about the agreement with Mr Nash for the remainder of the work. I trust to yours and William's judgement about it more than to myself, William thinks well of it and that it may in the end be the cheapest way of going to work and we both think Mr Nash to be trusted. I find on making Bevans take a more accurate measure of the Little Tower that it is lowered 5 inches ...'; but later a more ominous note appears in a letter of 1803 when she writes:[2] '... I always feared Nash was too moderate in his first valuations. I'm very anxious to know what he now makes it. I hope not more than £10,000 ...'.

The recent history of Killymoon is both sad and heartening. The demesne was cut up and sold in lots (mostly for its timber) in 1922, the part containing the castle being bought for a reputed £100 by the farmer who still owns it and has praiseworthily kept the fabric in serviceable repair ever since.

But the complicated and strife-ridden building of Killymoon was only a small part of Nash's story in Ireland, a fact he made quite clear to the Stewarts when he wrote in connection with a proposed visit:[3] '... I shall have business in Durham, consequently shall come by the short sea (route) and take Lord O'Neal in on my way to Killymoon and the Dowager Lady Longford ...'.

'Lord O'Neal' was Earl O'Neill, an eccentric bachelor with an ancient house set in seventy-five thousand acres at Randalstown, Co. Antrim. The land, thickly wooded and of great natural beauty, was bounded by the shores of Lough Neagh, the largest sheet of water in Ireland. It was Nash's job to add a south front and conservatory in Gothic style to

[1] The Clements Papers. [2] *Ibid.* [3] *Ibid.*

Shane's Castle with a great terrace overlooking the lough.[1] The work can be dated about 1810, but in 1816 the entire house was burnt down and all that remains of Nash's work is the embattled conservatory of thirteen round-headed bays, now filled with a remarkable collection of camellias. The terrace is much in the style of Caerhayes and East Cowes.

Due north of Belfast are the remains of Kilwaughter Castle, Co. Antrim, Nash's castellated house being an addition to a 17th-century castle on land owned by the Agnew family since the 12th century. Philip d'Agneaux was a Norman knight who came to Ulster in 1177 with John de Courcy; Nash's house was built for his descendant, Edward Jones Agnew, in 1807.[2] Even in its days of prosperity the house must have presented a melancholy face to this attractive piece of Ulster countryside. Here styles and materials were almost aggressively mixed up and the result was as bad as Killymoon was good. A massive round tower dominated the composition, but, at the end of the main block adjoining this and to the west corners of the old castle, Nash added corbelled turrets in caricature imitation of traditional Scottish style.[3] The walls were built of basalt blocks, cement-rendered, the windows dressed with pale hard buff sandstone and an oriel window to the north of the round tower was built of pinkish sandstone. The exterior details were a combination of flimsy Gothic fretwork to the windows, carried out in wood superimposed over the actual window frames and intricately carved sandstone window-sills of original and lively design applied to the new building and the old house. The interior was more carefully considered and there was some interesting plasterwork of fluted and vaulted spandrils; the entrance hall and staircase were panelled with thin wood Gothic tracery and there was a curved staircase at the north end. The round drawing room in the base of the tower was approached by a door contained in a coved semi-circular niche, one of a pair at the southern end of the semi-octagonal staircase hall. The house was stripped of its fittings and saleable materials in 1951, since when it has become a disintegrating shell.

While in the Antrim-Tyrone area Nash must have travelled constantly between Randalstown and Cookstown and there are many buildings, including churches, that might well be by his hand. Certainly he designed the not-very-distinguished parish church of Derryloran, Cookstown, of 1822;[4] it was built for £3,000 of which Colonel Stewart contributed £500. It is in simple Gothic with a pinnacled tower and plain spire and contains a vaulted vestibule. The church has been much altered and enlarged and it is probably only these features that are original. The nearby church at Kildress contains an attractive and elaborate plaster ceiling reputed to have been designed by Nash and of the same period.

[1] Information of Lord O'Neill.

[2] E. M. Jope, Professor of Archaeology, Queen's University, Belfast, has traced the history of the old castle and Nash's additions. See *Ulster Journal of Archaeology* (10), 1956.

[3] *See* illustration of the exterior in Davis: *op. cit.*

[4] There are sketches of the church by Nash at the Rectory, Cookstown, on paper dated 1814.

But, more important, is a building nearby of very different character—the third of the Italianate villas.

Originally set in its own secluded miniature parkland near Cookstown, Lissan Rectory is another example of Nash's patronage by the Stewart family, having been built in about 1806 for the Rev John Staples, son of a local squire and said to be a relation of the Stewarts. One would like to say that it is as good as Cronkhill and Sandridge, but it is merely a smaller and less successful version of both. Nevertheless it is unique in itself and possesses many attractive qualities. The plan of the main part of the house is rectangular and contains the drawing room, octagonal study, dining room and staircase hall.[1] The kitchen and other offices are strung out to the west and at the end of these is banished the round tower element common to all three Italianate houses; here it is not part of the main composition. As if to compensate for this, the square entrance porch to the north is quite impressive and contains a double front door with notable panels and spacious fanlight.

Fig. 11. Lissan Rectory, Co. Londonderry, 1807: the north elevation; the round tower is here isolated from the main block. From George Repton's Notebook (R.I.B.A.).

The decoration of the interior is entirely Classical and of high quality. All the original chimney-pieces have been removed, but the plasterwork mouldings and cornices survive, as do the prettily panelled shutters set in deep fluted recesses in the drawing room windows.

The south front contains a loggia of six arches supported on chamfered stone columns that leads off the drawing room and the study and originally had a shallow roof now replaced by a balcony. All the windows in the main block on this front are round-topped and the walls, now 'rough-cast', were stuccoed. It is altogether an unexpected and original house to find in rural Ireland.

In this neighbourhood at a later date Nash was busy at a much grander house, Castle Caledon, Co. Tyrone, the country seat of A. Du Pre, 2nd Earl of Caledon, who was Governor of the Cape of Good Hope from 1806 to 1811. The approach to the house is one of great beauty and variety made up of parkland, small valleys and clumps of magnificent

[1] There are plans and elevations in George Repton's notebook (R.I.B.A.).

25. Cronkhill, Shropshire, *c.* 1802: the earliest of the Italianate villas and the most arresting; the round tower is only a dramatic feature and is not essential to the plan.

26. Sandridge Park, Devon, 1805: the composition of round, square and linking elements is less successful here than at Cronkhill, but, as at West Grinstead, the shapes of the rooms are related to the exterior. The archway on the right is a modern replacement of a conservatory.

31. Castle Caledon: the library in the west pavilion with its dome decorated with diminishing paterae.

beeches and the house, built by Thomas Cooley in 1779, commands magnificent views on all sides. In about 1812 Nash added some important rooms on the ground floor, notably two square domed pavilions to the north front linked by a colonnade of coupled Ionic columns. At this time Nash was designing Park Crescent, Regent's Park, where he used the same columnar treatment. The west pavilion contains the library, a basically square room with a round dome containing diminishing paterae; giant Corinthian columns (used also at Attingham) are painted to imitate porphyry. The deep spandrels contain wreaths at each corner and the walls have elaborate plasterwork panels in which to contain royal and family portraits. The fireplace of white marble is on a heroic scale, Egyptian in taste and decorated with brass mounts. The oval drawing room is by comparison a plain room and contains curiously naive gilt paper silhouettes in panels and friezes. The room is vaguely Paris Directoire in flavour, and belongs to the Cooley plan, but may have been decorated by Nash. The south pavilion, now a bedroom, was originally a gun room. Though the rooms Nash added to the house are splendid it is doubtful whether they improved the exterior of the house. The Ionic colonnade with its flanking pavilions, although an attractive feature in itself, looks out of scale and the bedroom windows are truncated by the heavy balustrade; the whole feature reminds one of a Classical screen that has wandered up to the north front from some more suitable position in the park. After Nash's time a heavy portico was added to form a new entrance to the east and to the whole of the original centre block a complete storey was added.[1]

South-west of Caledon near the pleasant little town of Boyle in County Roscommon Nash was to build his most ambitious Classical house. The client was Robert Edward King, 1st Viscount Lorton of Boyle, a distinguished soldier and owner of one of the most spectacular and beautiful demesnes in Ireland. Rockingham overlooked panoramic views of lakes, valleys and thickly timbered parkland and was building in about 1809, in which year Lord Lorton wrote to Stewart of Killymoon:[2] '. . . I return you many thanks for your very kind letter of 21st, and further for the advice respecting the building you were so good as to give me, which, however (from various circumstances) I shall not be able to follow as I find that the best way *for me* will be to reduce the expense to a certainty and which Mr Nash will engage to do and also to finish the work in the very best manner possible; he has been here and we have made more alterations and a small reduction in the plan and which upon the whole very much improves it . . .'. Whether Nash's plan was modified or not in the end, a very splendid affair emerged and, contrary to Lord Lorton's desire to economise in 1809, he added two storeys in 1822 and completely upset Nash's original design. This consisted of a central round dome over a curved Ionic loggia at ground level, flanked by identical wings containing three round-headed windows set between Ionic pilasters at ground floor level;

[1] See *Country Life*, 27th February and 6th March, 1937.

[2] The Clements Papers.

the bedroom windows were square. Only the dome and loggia were balustraded, the plain parapets of the wings supporting pairs of sphinxes, a motif from Southgate. The whole was built of local limestone and was reminiscent of Holland's Pavilion at Brighton and Casina at Dulwich. The plan contained a circular library with other reception rooms on either side and the staircase hall was galleried and top-lit by three domed bays.

The house was badly damaged by fire in 1860, restored to its 1822 appearance and finally completely gutted by fire in 1957. Since then the demesne has been sadly neglected and much of its timber cut down. There are Nash-like cottages and lodges dotted about the vast estate and he may have done designs for the charming little Gothic church which stands isolated below the house, although this was not built until after his death.

A Gothic pile that shared many features with (and the same fate as) its cousin, Ravensworth, was Shanbally Castle in Co. Tipperary, due south of Rockingham. It was a rambling affair of great size built for the Earl of Lismore, the work supervised by A. Hargreaves. The original plans and elevations of this house at the R.I.B.A. are undated, but an approximate date might be 1814—about the same time as Lough Cutra Castle in nearby Galway was being considered and at a time when Nash was tied to London. The entrance front was like several of his other Gothic houses, but its *tour de force* was the south front—the great run of Gothic windows 'stopped' by the vast round and octagonal towers at each end with the only 'regular' section being in the centre of an irregular composition, comprising twin turrets and balanced fenestration. The rest of the elevation is made up of bay windows and a six-bay open loggia.

The interior was another example of Nash's concern with shapes and here we have an hexagonal dining room connected to an oval drawing room by a square ante room, thence a library, conservatory, smaller octagonal rooms, and to the east, a billiards room and other large rooms. The plasterwork was all Gothic and of good quality. The entrance hall was a long vaulted gallery, lit by a series of rose-shaped lay-lights and had an immense Gothic archway leading to the double-return staircase with oak balusters identical to those used at Lough Cutra.[1]

Neale[2] describes a 'picturesque and commodious residence'—the design 'furnished by Mr Nash of London'. This is Gracefield Lodge in old Queen's County (now part of Co. Kildare). The description accompanies a view of the house, the engraving of which must have been done from Nash's original design and not from the house itself which emerged as a very modest affair indeed, lacking most of the 'frequent breaks, and strong projections in the walls, the cut-stone labels surmounting the windows . . .'. The house was built by a Mr Robertson of Kilkenny for Mrs Kavanagh in 1817. Though much altered and reduced in size from the original plan, the house is attractive enough and set in lovely surroundings.

[1] *See* illustrations of the staircase and ceiling plasterwork in Davis: *op. cit.*

[2] J. P. Neale: *Views of the Seats of Noblemen and Gentlemen etc.* 6 vols. 1818–29.

It also provides us with the only example of Nash's 'Tudor' cottage-style villa in Ireland.

One of Nash's last clients in Ireland was Charles Vereker, Member of Parliament for Limerick who later became Lord Gort, taking his name from the small town in Galway near which he built his castle. It is said that Vereker so much admired Nash's own castle at East Cowes that he commissioned a similar one to be built on the shores of the lough in this remote and beautiful part of the country. In fact Lough Cutra Castle (*c.* 1815) is a much more compact design than East Cowes and basically it was quite small. The offices and gardens were created on an area blasted from solid rock so that the castle could be sited facing the views across the lough to the unspoiled and richly-timbered country beyond. The great tower contains an octagonal room, but the drawing room is rectangular linked with the dining room by a vaulted ante room. The hall is gallery-like once more, but on a modest scale and the staircase, housed in a circular tower on the entrance front, is pleasant but unspectacular.[1] The service wing is hidden behind trees and shrubbery to the east and built directly on to the solid crags. The building was carried out by George Richard Pain, an apprentice of Nash's practising at Cork, who also assisted at Shanbally. In 1856 Nash's composition was completely overwhelmed by massive additions in front of the service wing when Lord Gough of Goojerat fame had acquired the castle. He also removed most of the original fireplaces and thoroughly 'Victorianised' the interior. Nash designed furniture for the house and the pieces were stamped with his name, but these unfortunately have been dispersed. From 1922 until recent years the castle was unoccupied and semi-derelict, but it is now happily in the hands of the Vereker family once more.

Before Lough Cutra was finished Nash had virtually given up country-house design for good and although he may have visited Ireland after about 1812, it is unlikely that he would have spent much time over there with clients or hoping for new ones. By then the pattern of his working life had changed and he was embarking on the third and most spectacular part of his career. His private life, too, appeared to be settled; but we must return to the London of 1798 in order to look more closely into this.

[1] *See* illustration of staircase in Davis: *op. cit.*

CHAPTER FOUR

A Question of Marriage

THE first we have heard of Mrs Nash is in her husband's letter of 1802 to Mrs Stewart. She was Mary Ann Bradley, the daughter of an unsuccessful coal-merchant and had married Nash in December, 1798, at St George's, Hanover Square, possibly as his second wife.[1] He was forty-six, his bride twenty-five.

The Bradleys came from Worcestershire and were connected by marriage to the Worcestershire Pennethornes,[2] a name that was to become an integral part of the Nashes' lives at East Cowes. It is at this point that the true story of Mary Ann Bradley becomes obscure and presents the second mystery in Nash's life—whether his wife was one of the Prince Regent's mistresses. The fact that every scrap of evidence to prove one thing or another was deliberately destroyed only tends to encourage endless speculation, sometimes supported by legend and hearsay, sometimes by sheer guesswork. But if there was nothing to hide, why was everything so carefully hidden?[3] Was it merely rumour and malicious gossip that prompted the rollicking ballad, published about 1822, entitled *The Royal George Afloat?*[4]

She's[5] the people on her side, and that nobody can doubt,
Like a torrent in her cause they incessantly flow,

[1] Sir John Summerson has discussed the possibility of Nash having been previously married. (*See* Summerson: *op. cit.*, p. 76). Britton refers to Nash's 'second wife'.

[2] Originally 'Pennythorne'.

[3] The Duke of Wellington, the Prince's executor, may have destroyed most of the personal papers at the latter's death.

[4] There are six verses; above is a coloured cartoon of George IV embracing Mrs Nash and exclaiming: 'I have great pleasure in visiting *this part* of my dominions.' On the floor is a scroll reading 'The Loyal Address of Cows'. There is a copy at the Royal Pavilion in the Fetherstonhaugh Collection of Prints. *See* plate 37.

[5] Queen Caroline.

The dirty tricks of G——ge—oh! at last they are found out,
What the Devil I'm to do—only God himself can know.
In the boat with Mrs N-sh,
To the Isle of Wight I'll dash,
In my cabin smoke and drink, and forget I have a foe;
There's C——e my Wife,
She's the plague of my life,
And from her I'll make sail with a yo heave ho.

Now the Yacht it is all ready, for the Isle of Wight I'll steer,
With the lovely Mrs N-sh I am all upon the go,
I'll pack the husband off—for he has no business here,
With his Wife in pleasure's bark, I will jovially row.
In the Place of Waterloo,
He may fume, fret and stew,
'Tis an architects disgrace, and that the world does know,
Here at Cowes I will revel,
Kicking Virtue to the Devil,
With N-sh have a Smash, singing yo heave ho.

The facts of the case are that Mary Ann Nash when young was very attractive, if the portrait of her at the time of her marriage is a good likeness,[1] and that she brought up five children at East Cowes—Thomas, Anne, James, Sarah and John—all of whom were called Pennethorne. They were said to be grandchildren of her maternal grandmother's sister and Thomas, the eldest, was born at the time the Nashes married. Nash had or recognised no children of his own and made no provision for the Pennethornes in his will. Anne, Sarah and, later, John lived on at Hamstead (Nash's rustic country retreat near East Cowes) in considerable style until the death of Mrs Nash in 1851, surrounded by royal relics;[2] after that the money to keep up the house suddenly stopped, although the Pennethorne family

[1] One of a set of three miniatures of Mary Ann Nash, her sister Grace and John Nash in the possession of Mrs Neville Laing, great-grand-daughter of Sir James Pennethorne. *See* reproductions of the Nashes in Summerson, *op. cit.*

[2] There were several royal portraits at East Cowes. These, together with items of furniture and other relics, were removed to Hamstead and have since been dispersed amongst the Pennethorne descendants. An oil portrait of George IV from Lawrence's studio is in the possession of Mrs Neville Laing. A set of mahogany dining chairs inlaid with brass—a gift from the Prince—is in the possession of Mr Peter Laing, son of Mrs Neville Laing, as are a marble bust and life-size oil portrait of Mrs Nash in later years. Miniature bronze busts of the Nashes are in the possession of Miss Gwyneth Pennethorne. The remains of personal Nash-Pennethorne papers etc. (including Nash's diaries for 1832 and 1835), the property of Mr Laing, are at Sir John Soane's Museum. A diamond ring, the only surviving piece of jewellery given by the Prince to Mrs Nash, is in the possession of Miss Jacqueline Laing, daughter of Mrs Neville Laing.

continued to live there on a reduced scale until 1923. The possibility that the children were royal bastards has been denied and confirmed by successive generations of their descendants, largely depending on their attitude to illegitimacy, royal or otherwise.

Thomas, who was a gifted watercolourist, died young but left a legacy of many drawings of scenes of the Isle of Wight and the Worcestershire countryside.[1] A portrait of Anne[2] (probably by Richard Evans)[3] shows her to have been a pleasant-looking young woman and not unlike Mrs Nash and her brother John. James[4] became Nash's chief assistant and was knighted in 1870 after a successful career in architecture; he was coarse featured and in no way resembled the Prince or Mrs Nash. A portrait of John[5] by Evans shows him as a very good-looking young man with more than a hint of the Prince's features if the imagination is allowed to wander. John produced a scholarly and bulky volume *The Geometry and Optics of Ancient Architecture* published in 1878—his professional swan-song.

The mystery deepens, however, when we consider the more important question of Nash's position in the matter. Did he marry the Prince's mistress or did his wife become the Prince's mistress later? The Prince thought nothing of borrowing his friends' wives, but if Miss Bradley was already in the royal bed before she married Nash certain coincidences should be examined.

When Nash returned to London he was no richer than any other hard-working architect would have been, but immediately after his marriage he was able to afford not only an impressive mansion in Dover Street but also a large estate in the Isle of Wight; and, moreover, he appeared to have the money required to lead a life far above the station of his colleagues. His mode of life was bitterly criticised in a letter[6] to his rival, Soane, some years later: '. . . Who that goes to Hay Hill would dream of the corner of Russell Street,[7] and Your account of escape, and would cast a thought upon the marshes of Lambeth[8]

[1] Large sketch albums are in the possession of Mr Peter Laing in which there are drawings of East Cowes Castle at early stages of building.

[2] Oils, life-size, in the possession of Mr Peter Laing.

[3] (1784–1871) portrait painter and copyist; pupil and assistant to Lawrence, became Nash's favourite artist for carrying out personal commissions. *See* p. 78.

[4] *See* Pennethorne Hughes: *The Last State Architect* (*Country Life*, 22nd February, 1952). The article shows an engraving of Sir James Pennethorne and the author discusses the question of royal bastardy. Pennethorne made many contributions to the Victorian scene and his position in the history of architecture is now being more fully appreciated. Among his more notable works were: the remodelling of the shops in the Quadrant after Nash's colonnade was demolished in 1848; the western group of buildings additional to Sir William Chambers's work at Somerset House; additional rooms at Buckingham Palace (*see* p. 94); the London University Buildings in Burlington Gardens.

[5] Oils, life-size, in the possession of Mrs Neville Laing.

[6] James Spiller to Soane, 13th March, 1814. Reprinted in A. T. Bolton: *op. cit.*

[7] Nash's property in Bloomsbury Square.

[8] Nash's childhood background.

amidst the Circean voluptuousness of the Isle of Wight? Oh you must have observed how much is done by gratifying animal propensities, the lovers of good eating and drinking will be found to constitute a very large majority in the Pig Sty and the Palace, and in the intermediates; I have heard of much gourmandizing and drenching that the recital has created a vertigo; whence came the original supplies I wonder, and by what means are architectural compositions prepared under a sick headache.'

No shred of evidence survives to suggest that Nash was more than an official husband to his wife or that their relationship was anything but a marriage of convenience—more convenient at the outset, perhaps, to the Prince than to Nash. If a matrimonial charade of this nature was being played out, it is possible to attribute Nash's sudden rise to prosperity to a form of royal dowry. Did the Prince, even in those early days, see Nash as his architect and provide in one gesture a wife and a fortune with which to set him up for a future of exceptional privilege? If not, where did the money come from? For the establishment in Dover Street alone was no ordinary architect's house.

No 29, Dover Street was Nash's second attempt in London to introduce a façade entirely covered in stucco, but it was a very different affair from the ill-fated house in Bloomsbury Square; it was pretentious and eccentric, contrasting strangely with the earlier 18th-century houses in the street. He had originally rented the house next door, No 28, at £280 per annum (a high rent in those days, even for a substantial town house), but he let this when he acquired the adjoining site which faced the steep opening of Hay Hill 'so that my house will front you as you come up . . .' he wrote in 1796.[1] The elevation of No 29 was an amalgam of several of Nash's favourite elements—a central porch with coupled Ionic columns, round-topped windows on the first floor, round windows flanking rectangular sash ones above, and, rising behind a heavy balustrade, the attic storey we have seen at Llysnewydd. This element, whenever Nash used it, was really a series of dormer windows disguised as a single unit, in this case containing oval windows divided by Classical figures. It was certainly odd, but no odder in its different way than Soane's house in Lincoln's Inn Fields was to be. It was to be his 'shop-window' and showplace and doubtless several commissions resulted directly therefrom.

The interior was equally striking and very spacious. The ground floor comprised a large entrance hall with dining room at the rear; on the first floor the drawing room had three windows overlooking the street with a domed alcove at one end to provide added interest.[2] In the back wing of the house was a large library with Corinthian columns on pedestals and curved walls at each side of the fireplace. Beyond this was a small study with a domed closet and back stairs leading via a basement passage to a side street entrance and also directly up to the second floor. The second floor was given over entirely to drawing

[1] To J. G. Philipps. Cwmgwili MSS.

[2] *See* sketch plan in Summerson: *op. cit.*, p. 81.

offices where Nash and his staff worked for several years; the top floor contained the bedrooms. The house was mutilated in 1934, bombed in 1941 and entirely rebuilt after the War.

The year of his marriage was a particularly busy one domestically. To balance his house in Dover Street Nash had bought a plot of land on the Isle of Wight near the fashionable and lively resort of Cowes with its many villas and other buildings dotted about the hilly surroundings. He had visited the island several times since the early 1790s and must have been diverted by this idyllic spot with its animated views of sailing boats on the Medina. It was later to be patronised by society and the Prince Regent, so, yet again, Nash had placed himself in the centre of things.

East Cowes Castle began as the compact, fairly modest house that Charles Vereker admired and commissioned for Lough Cutra; but it was to become Nash's personal plaything. He was obsessed by it and during the thirty-five years in which he lived there he added to it, redecorated it several times and finally installed the vaulted gallery from his house in Regent Street, complete and intact. When all was lost in London he retired and lived there till his death.

Considering that Nash had given his services to the town of Newport when he designed the Town Hall, Barber's *Picturesque Illustrations of the Isle of Wight*, published a year before Nash's death, gives an uncharitable description of the benefactor's house: '. . . the general effect of this castle, with its surrounding woods, must be admitted to be imposing. On nearer inspection, it is seen to unite the features of the castellated mansion of a late date, with those of the baronial stronghold of a much earlier period; the former, doubtless for convenience, the latter for the sake of antiquated and striking appearance. Whether such a union be consistent with correct taste, is a question which Mr Nash should be more qualified to answer than ourselves: but in this, as in many other instances, we confess to have been but little struck with the propriety of machicolated towers frowning over the elegancies of domestic architecture. When time has divested a style of building of its objects and meaning, it should be either wholly laid aside, or, if adopted in the way of imitation, the imitation should be completed, and should admit nothing of the incongruous: an axiom this, which has been but little studied by the architect and proprietor of East Cowes Castle.'

The house cannot be compared with Nash's other Gothic buldings so diverse are its elements—even though, analysing the complex, it possessed the familiar selection of octagonal, round and square towers and turrets, castellated and arcaded loggias and a conservatory.[1] The details combined square-headed Tudor windows with round-headed windows and pointed Gothic arches; but the total effect was enormously successful—both picturesque and tough—an 'authentic' fortified Tudor mansion, but with all the refinements

[1] *See* sketch plan in Summerson: *op. cit.*, p. 84.

32. Rockingham, Co. Roscommon, *c.* 1810: Nash's largest Classical house in Ireland, later spoiled by alterations; from a drawing probably by George Repton in the possession of Sir John Summerson.

33. Shanbally Castle, Co. Tipperary, *c.* 1814: designed by Nash and built by A. Hargreaves, the house resembled Ravensworth and it contained a great series of rooms with excellent Gothic plasterwork.

38. 29, Dover Street, London, *c.* 1798: Nash's own house and drawing office on a site facing down Hay Hill.

39. East Cowes Castle, Isle of Wight, from 1798. Nash's country house viewed from West Cowes across the harbour; from a set of engravings by G. Brannon published privately by Nash from 1825.

of a more sophisticated age. It was to become a museum filled with the resident curator-architect's favourite trappings.

A tour through the interior was described by Farington[1] in 1817 when he was allowed to wander through the rooms with a party of friends. After passing through the circular staircase hall with its fluted walls and dome they entered the dining room 'very genteely set for dinner for 7 persons'. On the walls there were drawings of houses designed by Nash and the room was richly decorated with a cavetto cornice incorporating fluted, scaly ovolo and tassel motifs. A black marble fireplace was enriched with brass mounts.

In the drawing room (a room that would echo the French feeling at Caledon), linked by the usual ante room, Farington found Nash himself with company almost as part of the 'show', so he passed on after a polite exchange of bows to the library via the short conservatory. The library ceiling had acanthus enrichments of Gothic flavour painted in red, blue, green and gold[2] and according to Farington was 'well stored with books'. The library was connected with the top-lit billiards room by a room with a circular fluted dome situated in the octagonal tower. At the end of the long conservatory, probably added later (and later still narrowed in part by the insertion of the Regent Street gallery), was a square room known as the Regent's Room, but there is no evidence of the Prince having stayed there though he was a frequent visitor.

This interesting monument to Nash's personal taste fell into decay after the First World War and has since been demolished. The beautiful gardens, possibly laid out by Repton, have been destroyed and this once richly-timbered paradise is now a closely packed housing estate. A concrete road is called John Nash Avenue.

As if this palatial establishment were not enough, Nash purchased the manor of Ningwood, about five miles to the north of Cowes in 1806, and had also bought the tiny secluded hamlet of Hamstead on the highest hill on that part of the island where he farmed some land. The house at Hamstead was used as a shooting box and it was to become the favourite retreat of Mrs Nash and the mysterious Pennethorne children.

The Nashes' lives were certainly full at East Cowes; invitations to stay and enjoy the amenities of the beautiful island were freely given to friends. Entertainment was lavish and generous and Nash set a precedent of all time when the Prince Regent dined at the castle on July 13th, 1817, in a scene of great splendour. On that day Farington noted: 'At the Butchers much was said of the quantity of provisions which had been carried to Mr Nash's above East Cowes in consequence of the Prince Regent being expected there.' No architect before or since his time was to play host to his Sovereign on such a lavish scale; the bankrupt builder-speculator of Bloomsbury had come a long way.

[1] *Op. cit.*, Vol. VIII, p. 143 *et seq.*

[2] A fragment of the cornice in the author's possession shows the unburnished gilding and colouring to be crudely executed. The enrichments were made of papier-mâché by Bielefelds, who supplied decorations for the House of Lords, British Museum and other public buildings.

The castle was considered 'suitable rather to a *grand seigneur* than to an architect',[1] a slighting remark that overlooked the fact that at this stage of his life he was undoubtedly both. But it is frustrating not to know more about Nash's domestic life both on the Isle of Wight and in London. Was Mrs Nash a willing and competent hostess to the many people of all walks of life who visited their houses or were these duties thrust upon her as part of the possible 'bargain'? Her husband's life was busy in the extreme and there must have been long periods when he was away on his far-flung sites. Do we see her as a neglected wife (a letter to Mrs Stewart[2] vaguely suggests this) and one who found her husband's social activities a bore? That Nash enjoyed issuing lavish invitations to East Cowes is confirmed by many, but no letters have survived to throw light on the true relationship of this strangely disparate pair.

As a celebrated architect Nash naturally received various local commissions, notably the building of the Isle of Wight Institution (1811) and the Town Hall[3] (1814), both in Newport. They are Classical buildings of some distinction and both have arcaded colonnades supporting a central pedimented feature. He designed several cottages and lodges on estates around Cowes, a Gothic villa[4] and an eccentric Classical house at Bembridge, called Hillgrove.[5] Other buildings on the island, as yet unidentified, may be by his hand.

In 1805 when East Cowes Castle was in its early stages of building we see Nash not only as a successful country-house architect, but also as a man of property with royal patronage (and the largest purse in the Kingdom) just within easy reach. His country house commissions were to continue on and off until about 1815 when, as we have seen, he designed Lough Cutra. But he is now about to make his entry into the world of officialdom and, although he would be free enough to carry out his private commissions for some years yet, his future was to become increasingly complicated by the arduous business of getting plans through committees and government departments.

[1] *Diary of Philip Neumann* (edited by E. B. Chancellor) 1928, Vol. I, p. 4.

[2] In Clements Papers, N.L.I.

[3] Working drawings are in the Borough Surveyor's office. The Corporation passed a vote of thanks 'for the very elegant and masterly plans . . . which, in the most liberal and flattering manner, he presented to the Corporation'. Nash was elected a free burgess of the Borough (County Record Office, Isle of Wight).

[4] *c.* 1825 for Sir John Coxe Hippisley, Bart, and now incorporated in later buildings belonging to the Royal Corinthian Yacht Club.

[5] For the Earl of Ducie. The house is now in disrepair.

CHAPTER FIVE

London Transformed

IN 1806 Nash was appointed architect to the Chief Commissioner of Woods and Forests. This was a Treasury appointment and the salary of only £200 per annum was also to cover the services of an assistant, James Morgan. How this appointment came about we do not precisely know, but the Chief Commissioner, Lord Robert Spencer, was one of the Fox-Sheridan coterie with whom the Prince Regent associated and Nash's Whig leanings may have brought him into this company at an early stage. More important was that Nash was once more in the right place at the right time and the words 'Woods and Forests' heralded the greatest opportunity of his life—the planning of Regent's Park.

Earlier, at the time Nash was shaking himself free of his Welsh works, the Surveyor-General of His Majesty's Land Revenue, John Fordyce, had suggested that long-term plans should be made for the future of all the Crown's London estates and that a prominent architect should be consulted on property matters so that comprehensive planning could be implemented.[1] In particular he turned his attention to Marylebone Farm, the fields and parkland to the north of Portland Place, most of it leased to the Duke of Portland until 1811. He was authorised to offer up to £1,000 to any architect who could produce a plan for its development and even gave them a sensible guide as to what might be done, leaving the actual planning and design to the candidates, adding: 'It is to be hoped that from the known talents of some of the persons who have agreed to give their attention to this great National object, that this opportunity will not be lost and that something will be produced that will do credit not only to themselves but to the country.'[2] Fordyce's offer was made in 1793, but even by 1809 no scheme had been submitted. In the same year he died and no

[1] 1st Report of the Surveyor-General of H.M. Land Revenues, 1797.
[2] 4th Report; App. XV, p. 245.

successor was appointed; instead the Office of Land Revenue was combined with the Office of Woods and Forests with Lord Glenbervie[1] as Chief Commissioner.

With only a few months to go before the Marylebone lands reverted to the Crown, the Commissioners hastily summoned the architects of the combined offices to prepare plans. In the former Land Revenue Office were two architects, T. Leverton[2] and T. Chawner, who produced their own scheme for the development. It turned out to be a logical extension of the streets and squares already established to the south which would have almost covered the whole area to be developed; nothing new, nothing daring. Nash's plan, on the other hand, was revolutionary by comparison and allowed for picturesque country scenery in the Repton tradition, to be enjoyed by detached villas in the centre and by great terraces of houses round the periphery. We do not know whether or not the Prince saw both schemes before they were submitted to the Treasury, but it is not difficult to visualise a scene of the Prince and Nash meeting at Dover Street or Carlton House during these hectic days; days when it must have become increasingly evident that each saw in the other complementary talents and opportunities. Whatever went on behind the scenes, in July, 1811, the Commissioners recommended Nash's plans to the Treasury. After being told that he should modify the scheme to show fewer buildings and more parkland (the original schemes preserved in the archives of the Commissioner for Crown Lands are very much more picturesque and more densely packed with buildings), the scheme was approved in October of that year.

Apart from the detailed planning of the Park itself with its terraces of houses, villas, markets and landscaping, Nash could see that one of the most important aspects of the whole scheme was to link all this to Portland Place, thence by some means to the palace of Carlton House in St James's—a great plan that would provide not only lucrative property for the Crown purse but also a grand processional route between the two parks. As a corollary to the park plans Nash, Leverton and Chawner had been invited to consider this new southward street. Fordyce and James Wyatt had also explored the matter, but Nash was the only one to ignore their ideas of widening existing streets and to exploit the natural boundaries of Soho and Mayfair as the line of the new route.

Nash's proposals for the rebuilding and replanning of the West End in this connection make excellent reading and give an entertaining picture of London life in the early 19th century. It is hardly surprising that the Prince, the Commissioners and the Treasury were delighted with them. On the face of it, the report was thorough and it was bold. It contained references from architecture to sewers; vistas to statuary; fashion to class-distinction. We cannot here examine the report at length, which in any case was modified, but the following extracts referring to the siting and proposed appearance of Regent Street

[1] Sylvester Douglas, Baron Glenbervie (1743–1823).
[2] Architect of Bedford Square, 1775.

40. The Town Hall or Guildhall, Newport, Isle of Wight, 1814: the building remains substantially as designed; drawn and engraved by T. Barber for *Picturesque Illustrations of the Isle of Wight*, etc. 1834

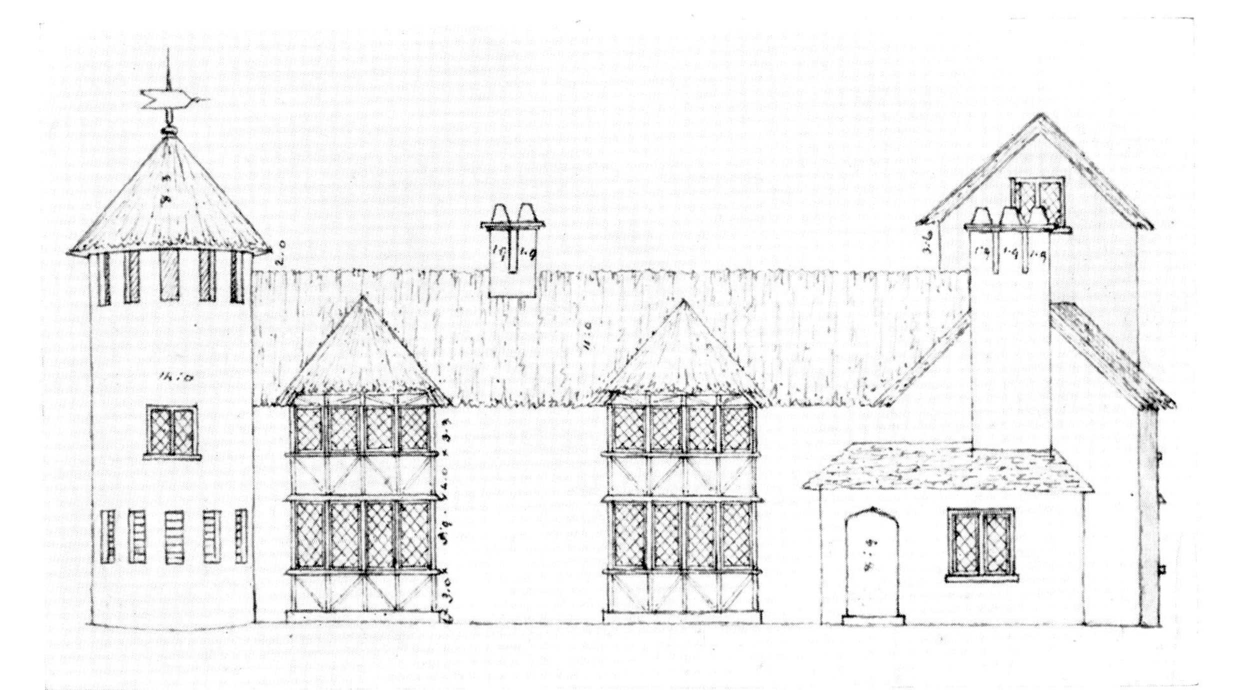

41. Hamstead, Isle of Wight, *c.* 1800: incorporating an old tower and used as a shooting box and later as the home of Mrs Nash and the Pennethorne children; from George Repton's Notebook (R.I.B.A.).

42. Hillgrove, Bembridge, Isle of Wight, undated: Nash designed several villas on the island; this one with its canted Ionic central feature is in disrepair and other have been demolished.

43. Park Crescent, Regent's Park, 1812–22: the sweeping colonnades adjoining Portland Place reach towards the greenery of the Park and herald the architectural scenery beyond.

44. Park Square, 1823: twin terraces north of Park Crescent were built when the plan to continue the crescent as a circus was abandoned. Drawn by T. Shepherd and engraved for Elmes's *Metropolitan Improvements*, 1827.

45. Ulster Terrace, 1824: a pair of terraces facing north at right-angles to Park Square. In the middle distance can be seen the Ionic terrace destroyed in the last War and next to it the Doric Villa (Elmes).

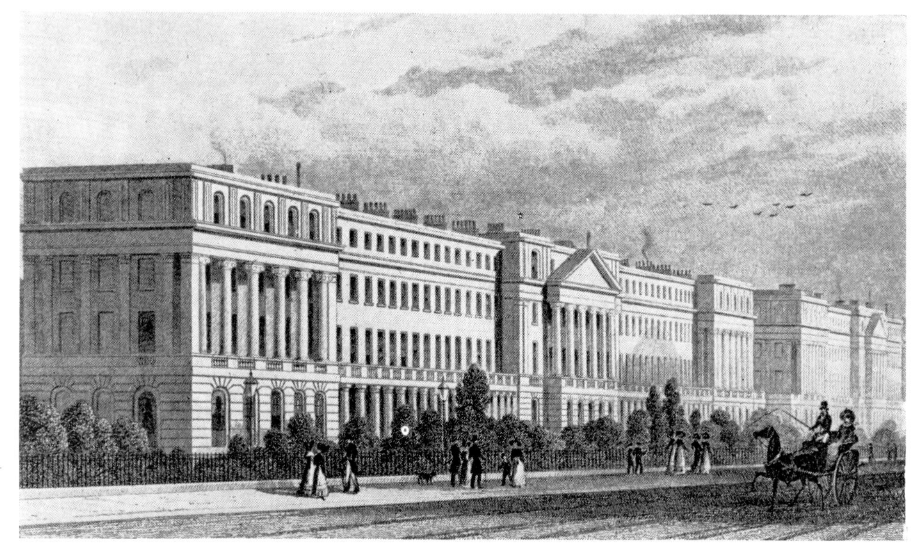

46. York Terrace 1822: a pair of massive terraces containing forty-nine houses (Elmes).

47. York Gate and St Marylebone Parish Church (Elmes).

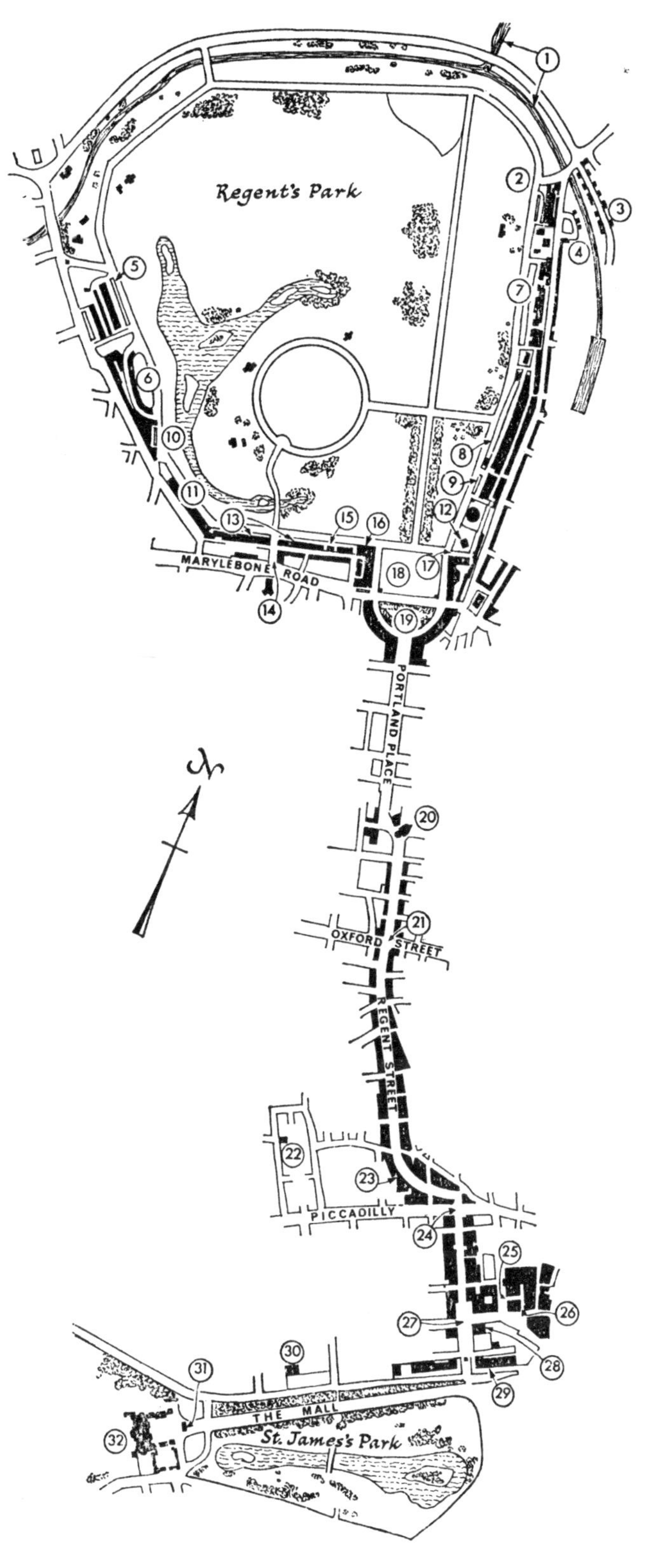

Fig. 12. Nash's London Developments, from 1812: *See* pp. 66–81.

1. The Regent's Canal
2. Gloucester Gate
3. Park Village East
4. Park Village West
5. Hanover and Kent Terraces
6. Sussex Place
7. Cumberland Terrace
8. Chester Terrace
9. Cambridge Terrace
10. Clarence Terrace
11. Cornwall Terrace
12. Someries House
13. York Terrace
14. York Gate
15. Doric Villa
16. Ulster Terrace
17. St Andrew's Place
18. Park Square
19. Park Crescent
20. All Souls' Church
21. Oxford Circus
22. 29, Dover Street
23. The Quadrant
24. Piccadilly Circus
25. Theatre Royal and Suffolk Place
26. Suffolk Street
27. Waterloo Place
28. United Service Club
29. Carlton House Terrace
30. Clarence House
31. The Marble Arch
32. Buckingham Palace

Nash also planned the area to the east of the Suffolk Street developments; i.e. Trafalgar Square and improvements to the Strand.

give its flavour. The new street would provide '. . . a boundary and complete separation between the Streets and Squares occupied by the Nobility and Gentry, and the narrow Streets and meaner Houses occupied by mechanics and the trading part of the community . . . those who have nothing to do but walk about and amuse themselves may do so every day in the week, instead of being frequently confined many days together to their Houses by rain . . . the Balustrades over the Colonnades will form Balconies to the Lodging-rooms over the Shops, from which the Occupiers of the Lodgings can see and converse with those passing in the Carriages underneath, and which will add to the gaiety of the scene, and induce single men, and others, who only visit Town occasionally, to give preference to such Lodgings . . .'.[1]

Nash's gay scene of young men chatting away from their balconies was not to last long, for in 1848 the colonnade of cast-iron Doric columns which in the end was built only in the Quadrant, was demolished and replaced by James Pennethorne's new shop-fronts and projecting balconies.

The First Report therefore was full of typical Nash enthusiasm. The enormous problems of instigating the plans, involving the purchase and demolition of existing buildings, some leasehold and some freehold, were to take care of themselves. Of course they didn't and Nash's life soon became a series of wranglings, protracted negotiations with owners and compromise. The critics of the scheme were soon demolished, but the negotiations necessary to implement the plans involving the new streets were endless.

Meanwhile the plans for the park were proceeding apace and the first building to emerge was Park Crescent in 1812—perhaps Nash's greatest single stroke of urban architecture. The New Road (now Marylebone Road) was a thoroughfare busy with constant traffic between east and west and this had to be disguised in some way in order to merge the fashionable mansions in Portland Place in the south with the new terraces of houses facing their own parkland further north. Perhaps it is curious therefore that cast-iron gates originally shut off the crescent from the New Road.[2] The original plan (in the First Report) was to place a vast circus of houses over the junction of the streets, but this was abandoned when the lessee became bankrupt and a crescent open to the park on the north was designed, the inviting greenery of the park being visible from the south end of Portland Place.

The great curved colonnades of coupled Ionic columns support a wide balustraded balcony at the first floor round-headed windows, the only decorative features in otherwise plain façades; but the houses at the ends of each quadrant have pediments flanked by Greek antifixae. The interiors of the houses were planned on traditional 18th-century lines

[1] 1st Report, p. 89.

[2] One pair of Greek Doric lodges formerly in the crescent gardens has been demolished for road-widening. The twin pair in Park Square has been moved to the north end of the square.

(as were all the houses in the park), but the interior plasterwork and sometimes the designs of the staircases were determined by the pockets and tastes of the first tenants. The cast-ironwork round the crescent gardens is of high quality and may have been designed by Nash. It was cast by Peachy who produced most of the railings, some still existing, in the park. The building of Park Crescent was not completed until 1820 and the remainder of the terraces were rising after 1812 until the last one, Gloucester Gate, was finished in 1827.

To the north of Park Crescent, Nash designed twin terraces, together known as Park Square—east and west. The terraces are again Ionic, but here the columns are not free-standing and the blocks are more elaborate and less satisfying than the simplicity of Park Crescent; but perhaps this was intended as a link from the latter to even more extravagant architectural scenes to come. The central portion of the east terrace contained the Diorama—a small theatre with a revolving stage set with two scenes which, by moving lights, gave realistic effects of sunlight, storms and so on. It was designed by Pugin when the terraces were begun in 1823.

At right-angles to the square facing north over the park is a twin pair of blocks known as Ulster Terrace, of 1824. They have Ionic columns at ground floor level and each has two sets of bow windows rising to the balustrades at attic level.

Travelling west on the southern perimeter of the park the first block was numbered 44–49, York Terrace. Of a solid Ionic character with an arcaded central feature it was entirely destroyed during the Second World War. Next to it and also numbered in the same terrace is a charming little house known as 'Doric Villa', in fact a pair of semi-detached houses. These modest houses, disguised as a Greek temple, serve as a gesture to the Picturesque and a welcome break from the phalanxes of neighbouring blocks.

Further to the west York Terrace of 1822 (built by James Burton under Nash) continues its immensely long façade to the opening of York Gate, after which a twin block completes the south side of the park. The blocks are bipartite and the order is Greek Ionic. The ground floor is rusticated and a Doric colonnade joins the outer blocks to the central pedimented feature. The blocks were designed to appear as two vast palaces facing their private parkland and the entrances to the individual houses are found in the mews at the back, the park façades uncluttered by such give-away features.

We now come to the first north-south feature since the splendour of Park Crescent—York Gate of about 1818. Here Nash paid Thomas Hardwick the compliment of making his new parish church the central feature of this successful piece of planning. Hardwick's church is imposing, a great Corinthian portico and an elaborate cupola surrounded by classical figures being the most salient features. It is built of stone and it is a tribute to Nash that the twin plaster façades of York Gate, involving Ionic pilasters, rustication, arcading and semi-circular windows, stand up to Hardwick's more substantial, serious building.

Next comes Cornwall Terrace (1820) facing north-east and forming the south-western corner of the park terraces. After Park Crescent it is the earliest of the terraces and was designed by Decimus Burton (son of James) under Nash's inspiration. It possesses all the qualities we expect of Nash and the nineteen houses contained in its long façade, broken by three Corinthian porticoes, the central one with giant freestanding columns, are terminated by a west front containing a bow window, its lights divided by four caryatids.

The next terrace after passing an entrance to the park from Baker Street is Clarence Terrace and is of a very different order. It was also built by James Burton in 1823 and here again his son is credited with the somewhat freakish design. The central block is linked to Corinthian pavilions by open Ionic colonnades, behind which are houses as an integral part of the block. Today, when much terrace architecture is uniformly dull, this terrace appears refreshingly original.

Familiar as the terraces are to all who study them, Sussex Place (1823) still comes as a surprise (and a welcome one perhaps) after all the plainer compositions surrounding the park. It is the tall domes that give us this surprise; remove them and we are left with a vast Corinthian palace, this time with curving outer wings terminating in pairs of octagonal towers. All the familiar elements are there, but Nash has juggled about with them and provided twenty-six houses, some of the more fortunate ones with octagonal rooms—and domes. James Elmes,[1] architect and arch-critic, in his *Metropolitan Improvements or London in the Nineteenth Century*, gives us a personal opinion of the terrace describing it as 'a singular contrast to the chaster beauties of the other terraces'; but other critics condemned it harshly. Today it remains an object of curiosity; in those days nothing short of the Classical tradition would please Londoners, even if supplied by Nash's lively hand.

As if to stress the importance of contrast, the next block is Hanover Terrace comprising twenty houses and here the pediments of the three Roman Doric porticos are filled with Classical sculpture. The rusticated ground floor arcade is very deep and therefore the front doors to the individual houses are scarcely visible. The terrace was built by J. M. Aitkens in 1822–23. Backing on to Hanover Terrace is Kent Terrace of 1827, the only block in the scheme not to face the park. It is a plain Greek Ionic composition gaining its effect from wide recessed arches containing very broad windows.

Until we reach Gloucester Gate directly opposite Hanover Terrace on the east side of the park, the outer perimeter is taken up by the Regent's Canal. In his original proposals Nash had suggested that a canal should run through the park in connection with the already established Paddington Basin, to provide his ornamental lakes with water and adding a picturesque note to the landscaping. With the Prince's approval of the idea and with an eye

[1] Elmes was one of Nash's fairest critics. *Metropolitan Improvements* gives descriptions of most of his London works and engravings from drawings by Thomas H. Shepherd show views of the terraces and the Regent Street buildings. The book was dedicated to the King in 1828. For other perambulations round the park *see* Summerson: *op. cit.* and Pevsner: *op. cit.*; 'London, B.E. 6', 1952.

to business, Nash formed a company to promote the cutting of the canal, the estimated cost being £280,000, with an annual revenue from traffic of £43,000. Nash purchased the maximum holding of fifty £100 shares and his wife held a further fifty shares. Other major shareholders included Lord Stanhope, Sir Thomas Bernard, George Nettleship, Lyndon Evelyn and the Duke of Gloucester. After long-drawn-out setbacks from which Nash suffered financially, the canal was opened in 1820.[1]

Until the canal basin was filled in (1942–43) the canal left the park at Gloucester Gate and threaded its way between the park villages east of Albany Street. The villages were not laid out until the mid-1820s and most of the villas were built at the time Nash was embroiled in the Buckingham Palace complications. No doubt he indicated the general layout and effect of the villages and left the designing of the individual villas to his chief assistant, James Pennethorne, to whom he assigned his practice in 1834.

We now travel south and come to the first terrace on the west side of the park. It is Gloucester Gate comprising eleven houses, to the north of which are several separate houses, numbered in the terrace, and the exit from the park to Camden Town. The terrace was started in 1827 by R. Mott, whose architect, J. J. Scoles, did not care for Nash's façade and proceeded to alter the size of the mouldings, resulting in a cornice entirely out of scale with the Ionic columns and lower part of the elevation, thus proving that once Nash's elements are altered in any way other faults are high-lighted. On seeing the finished building Nash made his now famous remark that 'the parts looked larger than he expected'.[2]

In complete contrast to the stuccoed terraces is St Katharine's Hospital, of stock brick with Tudor details. It was designed by Ambrose Poynter, one of Nash's pupils, and comprises a central church flanked by pensioners' accommodation.

Although Nash's original plans for the park were far more elaborate than those executed, a grandiose composition was always intended to be the most important feature of the eastern perimeter as it was to have faced the Prince's *guinguette* or pleasure pavilion. The *guinguette* was never built, but the site reserved to face it was still to contain Nash's most palatial gesture: Cumberland Terrace. William Mountford Nurse was the builder and the terrace was started in 1826 with James Thompson[3] as the architect. For all its faults of poor detail and deceit (the massive central pediment is not a gable-end) the total effect of the three great Ionic blocks linked by triumphal arches is magnificent. There have been, and always will be, critics of Bubb's sculpture in the pediment and on the balustrades, the urns and other decorative details; but that is to miss the point of Nash's *only* aim—to impress; to provide a terrace of houses that look nothing like houses; to design a great

[1] For a detailed account of the canal undertakings see Herbert Spencer: *London's Canal*, 1961.

[2] Summerson: *op. cit.*, p. 193.

[3] A pupil of J. B. Papworth and, like his master, produced his own book on cottage design. He may have helped with the design of one of the detached villas in the park, Albany Cottage (demolished).

theatrical façade, behind which were houses such as rich Londoners had lived in for nearly a hundred years in streets and squares, but never before in a park. It is surprising that Nash did not place the front doors of the individual houses at the rear of the blocks as he had done in several other of the terraces in order to preserve the palace illusion in his most palatial composition; but the doors are unobtrusive and disappear well enough into the ground-floor fenestration.

The next block is Cumberland Place, an isolated block of four houses of Corinthian order entered from the rear, behind which is Chester Place, a modest terrace of small houses of Tuscan character set back and with entrances in Albany Street.

Further south is Chester Terrace, the longest unbroken terrace in the park. Instead of using triumphal arches as a linking device in this vast Corinthian composition, here they are set at right-angles at each end and twin blocks of houses join them to form detached pavilions. The terrace was built by James Burton in 1825.

Cambridge Terrace was also built in 1825 by Mott and has no dominating architectural style; it resembles some of the Regent Street blocks with round-headed windows and incised pilasters.

Cambridge Gate, a heavy stone block of 1875, replaces Decimus Burton's Coliseum, a large domed building used for assemblies and exhibitions. Next to the Coliseum was the Adult Orphan Asylum (known as Someries House), now demolished, a square building which Nash designed without charge as an altruistic gesture; it was set in a large garden. Next door a pair of houses, disguised as a single Corinthian-porticoed villa of some pretension with entrances in Albany Street and the park, are set back in St Andrew's Place.

This brings us to the east twin block of Ulster Terrace, thence Park Square East at right-angles and the sweep of Park Crescent to complete the tour of the park buildings.

The area to the east of Albany Street was to be devoted to markets and the dwellings of tradesmen and artisans round the old canal basin. Nash himself became leaseholder of much of this land, and many of the squares and streets, although modest, had much charm. Munster (formerly York) Square was the most attractive and comprised small stuccoed houses with round-headed windows and excellent ironwork.[1] Great damage was done to this area in the Second World War and blocks of council flats have since been built over Nash's sites.

In Albany Street itself a long, low building numbering Nos 152–4 may be ascribed to Nash and was built on land leased to himself. It was one of his more modest investments and was built originally as an ophthalmic hospital for soldiers blinded in the Egyptian campaigns. The main elements were severely Greek in feeling and the central archway was surmounted by a columned cupola.[2]

[1] Illustrated in Rasmussen: *London—the Unique City*, 1937, p. 261.

[2] Illustrated in Davis: *op. cit.*

Several of the park terraces were severely damaged during the War and in 1947 the Government considered their future.[1] In June, 1962, the Crown Estate Commissioners announced a complete scheme for the preservation of the terraces designed to give the buildings at least a further sixty years of useful life.[2]

Between 1812 and 1821 Marylebone Park would have been a scene of desolation and disorder. The landscaping itself was an elaborate and complicated undertaking; trees that were planted took several years to enhance the surroundings; the basin for the ornamental water had to be excavated; and scaffolded terraces at various stages of building rose from seas of mud in the sites round the park. As we have noted, the Regent's Park we know today is but a fragment of Nash's original plan and although he may have been frustrated that only eight of the proposed twenty-eight detached villas in the park were allowed (none of which he personally designed), it was a tribute to his vision that the Commissioners halted more building in 1826 which they said might 'destroy the scenery and shut out the many beautiful views towards the Villages of Highgate and Hampstead . . .'.[3] At first, when the scheme was merely a discouraging sight of expensive building, Nash was heavily criticised; the revenue was little or nothing but, by 1821, when the first terraces were completed, the houses were let immediately and the Treasury was delighted with its net revenue of £13,624.

When tastes changed in the middle of the century and the demand was for heavy exteriors and dark, oppressive interiors, the terraces miraculously escaped mutilation. Extra storeys were added here and there; glazing bars were replaced by sheets of plate glass and interior details were smothered by Victorian decoration; but the basic scheme remained unchanged, the park increased in beauty and the houses, as Nash foretold, increased in value and desirability.

Few of the contemporary architectural pedants were able or charitable enough to overlook the slipshod details and appreciate the planning as a whole. Some of them, like Soane, were still busy perfecting their own personal styles or, like Elmes, concerned with analysing the terraces as individual disasters or successes. Nash was criticised for his use of stucco even though country buildings had been cement-rendered in similar fashion throughout the 18th century. It took the acute and observant eye of a travelling foreigner, Prince Pückler-Muskau, to let criticism of detail take second place to an appreciation of the park as a whole. In 1826 he wrote to his wife:[4] 'London is, however, extremely improved in the direction of Regent Street, Portland Place and the Regent's Park. Now, for the first time it has the air of a seat of Government (Residenz) and not an immeasurable metropolis

[1] The Gorell Committee.

[2] The Future of the Regent's Park Terraces: 3rd Statement by the Crown Estate Commissioners, June, 1962. HMSO.

[3] 5th Report, p. 11.

[4] *A Regency Visitor*: the letters of Prince Pückler-Muskau, edited by E. M. Butler, 1957, p. 38.

of "shop-keepers", to use Napoleon's expression. Although poor Mr Nash (an architect who has great influence over the King, and is the chief originator of these improvements) has fared so ill at the hands of connoisseurs,—and it cannot be denied that his buildings are a jumble of every sort of style, the result of which is rather "baroque" than original—yet the country is, in my opinion, much indebted to him for conceiving and executing such gigantic designs for the improvement of the metropolis. . . . It's true, one must not look too nicely into the details. . . . Faultless, on the other hand, is the landscape-gardening part of the park, which also originates with Mr Nash, especially in the disposition of the water. Art has here completely solved the difficult problem of concealing her operations under an appearance of unrestrained nature. You imagine you see a broad river flowing on through luxuriant banks, and going off in the distance several arms; while in fact you are looking upon a small piece of standing, though clear, water, created by art and labour. So beautiful a landscape as this, with hills in the distance, and surrounded by an inclosure of magnificent houses a league in circuit, is certainly a design worthy of one of the capitals of the world; and when the young trees are grown into magnificent giants, will scarcely find a rival. . . .'

Long before these words were written, Nash was of course firmly established in royal favour and they echo the Prince Regent's sentiments on first seeing the proposals when he is said to have declared that he was 'so pleased with the magnificent plan, it will quite eclipse Napoleon'.[1]

The first terraces in the park were well under way before the plans for Regent Street had gone through the highly complicated and long-drawn-out negotiations involved. By comparison the park was an easy planning matter; new buildings were going up on hitherto unbuilt-up land and the only main practical problem was to find builders and backers like W. M. Nurse, who were prepared to take leases of whole sites or single houses from the Commissioners at an agreed annual rental and make what they could of 'selling' sub-leases of the houses to tenants, who appreciated the virtue of Nash's scheme as it developed. Regent Street was quite a different matter; Nash now had to consider in detail the proposals set out in his *First Report* for the new street. The first plan, that of continuing Portland Place to Oxford Street, thence via a circus to continue south in a straight line cutting off Soho to the east and Mayfair to the west, was accompanied by two cheaper schemes, one of which showed the street to be curved. The curve was an alternative to a great square containing a monumental public building just north of Piccadilly. The curved plan was cheaper and promised the highest revenue in relation to the outlay. Nash's estimate was £330,754 1s. 1d. and the plan was accepted. The Treasury ordered a Bill[2] to go before Parliament and on June 5th, 1813, it was debated. There was some

[1] T. Moore to James Corry, October 24th, 1811.

[2] 'An Act for making a more convenient Communication from Mary-le-bone Park and the Northern Parts of the Metropolis, in the Parish of Saint Mary-le-bone, to Charing Cross within the Liberty of Westminster; and for making a more convenient Sewage for the same.'

opposition to the scheme, largely on the grounds of expense, but the Bill was passed and received royal assent on July 10th. Apart from forging the new street the Act allowed for the widening of streets south of Piccadilly and the planning of what was later to be known as Trafalgar Square. The scheme was largely financed by an insurance company and when more money was required it came from the Bank of England.

To join Park Crescent to existing Portland Place was easily and successfully accomplished, but once south of Portland Place there were obstacles in the way and Nash was unable to continue the street due south as he wished. There were two reasons for this; Sir James Langham was leaseholder of a property at the south-west corner of Portland Place in direct line with the new street. (Nash had earlier, in one of his speculative moods, purchased the lease of the site from an old debtor, Lord Foley, for whom he had made extensive alterations at Witley Court, Worcestershire.)[1] As it turned out the street could never have been straight at this point as the backs of the houses in Cavendish Square would have been encroached upon, but Upper Regent Street could have been joined to Portland Place in a wide sweep had Langham been prepared to have the backs of the buildings in the new street directly overlooking his property. He was not and paid a vast sum to purchase the land running from his house to the line of the new street.

Thus the new street was pushed eastwards and all Nash's ingenuity was required to put matters right. His solution was to place his new church, All Souls', Langham Place, at an angle on the south east corner of Portland Place, the main body of the building out of sight when viewed from the south and its circular portico, peristyle and spire closing the vista. The spire alone tells us that it is a church; had the peristyle been domed it would have served the same purpose, that of a brilliantly placed feature; a temple; a folly.

The church, of Bath stone, was ridiculed when it was built (1822–24); and no-one appears to have appreciated its importance in the planning of the street. Today this function has been totally eclipsed; the much-criticised spire is lost against the towering blocks of the British Broadcasting Corporation (hopelessly out of scale with Portland Place in the first place) and Sir James Langham's garden opposite has long been replaced by the ponderous hulk of the Langham Hotel, interesting enough in our eyes today, but more suited to the architectural scenery of an important railway station.

The junction of Regent Street and Oxford Street was easily solved by a circus;[2] but at planning stage even this was objected to on the grounds that it would spoil Oxford Street. It is difficult today to imagine a more logical solution.

Unlike the Regent Street of today, Nash's street was visualised as part-residential, part-commercial. The northern part of the street, close to Portland Place (which was, of course, entirely residential) contained several houses, but lower down towards Piccadilly and

[1] Nash's Ionic portico is illustrated in Davis: *op. cit.* There are large water colour drawings at the R.I.B.A.

[2] Originally known as the Regent's Circus.

further south, individual town houses gave way to buildings designed as what are today called 'shop and upper part'. The ground-floor shops were the main source of revenue, but above them were apartments, equivalent to our flats or bachelor rooms of today, depending on how the lessee of the building decided to recoup his capital outlay. Nash bore the responsibility of organising the financial side of the scheme and was heavily involved personally with the leases in the Quadrant adjoining Piccadilly Circus. He took the responsibility of being the leaseholder of all the Quadrant sites comprising two curved blocks in order to ensure that the composition turned out as he wished and only secondarily that he might profit from the experiment. The ground rent, of course, went to the Treasury.

The Quadrant blocks were built by a group of tradesmen employed by Nash on the understanding that each took a house (or several houses), paying Nash for the building plus a five per cent commission. The tradesmen were plumbers, bricklayers and others connected with the building trade. In order to get the scheme started Nash lent them money to pay for the building and their debts to him were wiped out by the work and materials they supplied in the Quadrant and elsewhere.[1] The highly involved book-keeping this arrangement necessitated can be imagined and the squabbles and misunderstandings must have been incessant. It is said that Nash lost heavily on the deal and here we may credit him with being mainly concerned with aesthetics; and, if financial loss was involved, there would be other opportunities, he hoped, to speculate to his own advantage. It was not until some time later that the Quadrant fulfilled its true aim: to attract prominent shopkeepers from the City and St James's to this newly-fashionable centre.

As soon as the Regent Street developments were seen to be successful the Commissioners asked Nash to continue his plans eastwards and to connect the new work to the British Museum in isolated Bloomsbury.[2] To Nash we owe the existence of Trafalgar Square (though he designed no buildings in it) as a suitable termination to Whitehall and the widening of the Strand where Smirke's domed buildings at the corner of King William Street and Adelaide Street still exist to remind us of the old Vigo Street–Regent Street terminal. To link Trafalgar Square (so named in 1830) to Bloomsbury, Nash proposed a broad, straight street following the line of St Martin's Lane and joined by a widened Coventry Street east of Piccadilly. The latter idea was carried out at a much later date, but the St Martin's Lane plan was never adopted and when Charing Cross Road and Tottenham Court Road were developed in the 1880s, the British Museum was to remain marooned from the West End for ever.

Looking at old prints of Regent Street we are apt to think of it as a series of quasi-Classical blocks making up a fairly balanced 'Regency' thoroughfare with the Quadrant as

[1] Nash's ledger, discovered at Shide, Isle of Wight in 1932, gives details of these complicated transactions. Christened the 'Shide Ledger' by Sir John Summerson, it is now at the R.I.B.A.

[2] 5th Report, p. 12.

its most spectacular element.[1] In fact it was nothing of the sort; the blocks, Ionic, Corinthian, astylar, elaborate or plain, provided a progress of great variety and were sometimes interspersed by a church, an assembly hall, an hotel or other non-terraced buildings. The great sweep of the Quadrant did not, at the Vigo Street crossing, abruptly join the hard lines of further buildings; the vista formed by the arms of the Doric colonnades was closed by a domed Corinthian rotunda on the southern end of the next block, fulfilling a similar purpose to that of All Souls' Church and inviting the eye round the corner to other architectural scenes.

These set pieces were determined as to length and style partly by what sites were available, partly by prospective clients' wishes and, more important, by a genuine desire to break away from the formal street architecture of the 18th century. The skyline was irregular; Nash was using formal façades in an informal manner; here was an attempt to unite the Classical with the Romantic. He was creating the first deliberately Picturesque street in London and to analyse each building for faults of detail is, as with the park terraces, to overlook the main point of the plan.[2] In fact the buildings varied considerably in architectural quality and not all were designed by Nash. C. R. Cockerell designed Hanover Chapel at Hanover Street with its great stone Ionic portico; Soane designed a singular block north of Beak Street (on the side of the street screening the squalor of Soho); Burton, G. S. Repton, Smirke and other less prominent architects and builders designed further blocks. The business of co-ordinating this medley of designs and designers was Nash's and at the outset it was he who was responsible for providing the Commissioners with plans and estimates for drainage, sewers[3] and the buying-up of property not owned by the Crown (especially that on the east side of the street) in order to cut the new thoroughfare. By 1819 nearly one million pounds had been poured into these preparations by the Treasury (double the figure Nash had estimated solely for the purchase of goodwill) and for three years from 1815 commercial chaos and Government doubts were Nash's everyday companions. The physical disorder was on a greater scale than Londoners had ever known and the inconvenience caused by these great building operations was, of course, another weapon to be used against Nash by envious colleagues and laymen alike. The Regent Street development shared a common problem with the Regent's Park scheme: to encourage fashion to 'cross the road', in this case the eastern end of Piccadilly. The north-south Bond Street was old established as a commercial centre of the fashionable West End, but Regent Street was something new; it took time. But after many set-backs the slow surge to acquire premises

[1] Engravings and lithographs were produced by T. H. Shepherd and T. S. Boys; many original drawings and photographs of the buildings are in the archives of the Crown Commissioners, others in the Crace Collection, British Museum.

[2] The medieval precedent was Oxford High Street (quoted by Nash) where picturesque unity was achieved by linking a number of diverse buildings. *See* Summerson: *op. cit.*, pp. 202–03.

[3] Nash's first estimate for a new sewer was £54,000.

in the new street began and by 1819 rents were coming in to the Crown coffers from various buildings along its great length.[1]

Piccadilly Circus with its Ionic pilasters dividing shop windows and incised pilaster strips decorating the upper parts, joined the Quadrant skillfully to the lower part of Regent Street at the southern end of which was Carlton House.[2] The Prince's early eighteenth-century palace embellished with Holland's Ionic screen and Corinthian portico.

Commercially, this lower part was an easier proposition; any building in St James's had always been suitable for letting and the nearer to Carlton House and St James's Palace the better. Much of the land belonged to the Crown and the area that concerned Nash was traditionally the home of mens' clubs, important offices, hotels and banks. It was close by St James's Square, long-inhabited by the aristocracy and the very rich. This lower part of Regent Street, therefore, was a mixture of official and commercial offices interspersed with houses and one or two large private mansions, hotels and a church. At the upper end two symmetrical blocks adjoined the southern quadrants of Piccadilly Circus; looking north across the circus the vista was closed by the County Fire Office built in 1819—a grandiose Corinthian building with arcaded ground floor—a building considered worthy to face Carlton House down the hill and derived from the south elevation of Inigo Jones's Gallery at Somerset House. It adjoined the south-east end of the Quadrant and its façade formed the northern side of a small square to the south of which was the Circus itself—another example of Nash's ability to turn planning difficulties into features of positive value.

The southern end of Regent Street was opened out to form virtually another square known as Waterloo Place (built by James Burton who proved to be Nash's great supporter in the developments), soon to rival St James's Square owing to its proximity to Carlton House. The 'square' was strictly formal, comprising large houses of Classical character with Ionic porticos—in contrast to the picturesque selection of buildings to the north giving way to planned symmetry again only at the flanks of the Circus quadrants.

The house that should interest us most here was numbered 14–16 Regent Street,[3] just north of the Carlton Street crossing; a great Classical town house of imposing appearance with a spacious forecourt and projecting wings, it almost rivalled Carlton House; it was Nash's new London home.

But before we look more closely at this important building we must introduce the elusive figure of John Edwards; the Regent Street house was so designed that he and Nash

[1] Nash's Regent Street was destroyed in the 1920s largely owing to the high potential of its commercial siting (the park terraces, being entirely residential, were conversely spared). 'The true and sad story of the Regent's Street' is told in Rasmussen: *op. cit.*, chap. XI. A detailed survey of the street is given in Summerson: *op. cit.*, p. 202 *et seq.*

[2] Nash's clever planning at this awkward junction became a shapeless mass when his Circus quadrants were demolished.

[3] There is a fine watercolour of the house in the possession of Mrs Laing.

shared the spaciously-planned domestic accommodation. Edwards's true identity represents another major mystery in Nash's life. He was a lawyer who was concerned with the legal side of the building of Sir Edward Winnington's bridge at Stanford. He was born in Lambeth in 1772 and his family, like Nash's, appear to have been mill-wrights in Lambeth. Without knowing all the facts any number of theories may be woven round the possibilities. The known facts are that Nash was on close personal terms with Edwards all his life; Nash willed almost his entire estate to Edwards's son; Edwards was known by contemporaries variously as Nash's 'relation', 'uncle' or 'nephew'; Nash introduced him to Philipps of Cwmgwili as his cousin;[1] George IV called him Nash's nephew;[2] Farington called him his 'relation'.[3] He changed his name to 'Vaughan' after inheriting Rheola, near Neath, a modest house which Nash enlarged and remodelled;[4] he was involved by Nash in certain building projects, notably the ill-fated Regent's Canal and Suffolk Street affairs, and he and his family eventually lived in the house in Bloomsbury Square, the scene of Nash's first disaster.

We can colour the picture a little by adding that Edwards married two heiresses and that when Nash was interesting him in property speculations there would have been plenty of money available. They were probably friends and collaborators from early London days, foreseeing that their lives would be somehow bound up in the future. Perhaps Nash saw Edwards as the useful and astute lawyer he was to become and introduced him to the Stanford Bridge business of 1795 as a foretaste of better things to come. In any event Edwards left a great fortune to his son who was christened Nash Vaughan Edwards Vaughan. Descendants of the Vaughans recognise no relationship to Nash.

The leases of the sites on which the Regent Street house was built were taken in 1818–19 and the house was completed by 1824. By then Nash was seventy-two and Edwards fifty-two; Nash was to outlive Edwards by two years. Doubtless he persuaded Edwards to invest in this property in order that he could devise for himself a London setting more suited to the most celebrated architect of the day. Like most of Nash's buildings in the new street it was planned to accommodate more than lavish living quarters. The ground floor was devoted to shops, offices and stables bringing in a useful revenue, or at least covering the outgoings of rent to the Crown and some of the runnng costs—the principle on which the whole of the commercial parts of the new street was based. It was another example of Nash's talent for handsomely disguising several components as a single unit. Edwards

[1] Writing from 30, Duke Street in 1796 to Philipps he said: '. . . let me recommend my cousin John Edwards, No 5, New Inn. You know him . . .' (Cwmgwili MSS).

[2] *See* letter to Wellington, p. 97.

[3] 'Mr Nash described to me the gallery he had built in Regent Street. Mr Edwards, his relation, had united with him in building the houses in that street, each of them to have one. The Houses join and to his Mr Nash has joined a gallery. He said they had expended £39,000 . . .' (*op. cit.*, entry from 5th November, 1821.)

[4] There are drawings of estate buildings in George Repton's notebook (Royal Pavilion).

occupied No 16, the northern end of the building, and his first-floor rooms, reached by a circular staircase, comprised a circular columned ante-room, long gallery and inter-communicating drawing and dining room. The main part of Nash's accommodation was on the first floor of the south wing and, apart from the kitchen which was below in traditional style, he designed for himself the first self-contained flat in London. It was, in fact, a suite of rooms in which to display his status, his taste and himself. They were not the rooms of a connoisseur-collector or scholar such as were Soane's in Lincoln's Inn Fields—they were the rooms of a showman, rich and glittering and filled with specially commissioned copies of paintings by Titian, Caravaggio and others.[1] A bedroom, dressing room and bathroom were squashed to one side, thus allowing a regal progress to be made from front to back of the building through an ante-room, square drawing room, the famous gallery (seventy feet in length) and rectangular dining room. A further ante-room led to a 'Gallery of Architecture'.

While Nash lived here his private practice was almost over and the bulk of his work was of an official nature, many of his staff being accommodated in the Commissioners' offices and elsewhere. But although the Regent Street rooms were designed and used mostly as a showplace, drawing office accommodation was provided in a top-lit room off the dining room. Nash may have kept on the Dover Street house as offices after 1824, but we know that he was trying to let it to Edward Bulwer (later Lord Lytton) in 1829.[2]

Nash was inundated with requests to see his gallery and among his visitors in 1824 was the King. Two years later the insatiably curious Prince Pückler-Muskau was again on the scene and gave the following description of the place:[3] 'I have paid several visits to Mr Nash. . . . He is said to have "erected" an enormous fortune. He has a beautiful country-house, and no artist is more handsomely lodged in town. I was particularly pleased with his library. It consists of a large long and wide gallery, with twelve deep niches on each side, and two large doorways at the ends, leading into two other spacious rooms. In each niche is a semi-circular window in the roof, and on the wall a fresco painting copied from the 'Logge di Rafaelle'; and below these, casts of the best antique statues, on pedestals. The remaining space in the niches is occupied by books which, however, rise no higher than the pedestal of the statues. Arabesques, also copied from those of the Vatican, admirably executed in fresco, adorn the broad pilasters between the niches.

'All the space on the walls or pilasters not covered with paintings is of a pale red stucco, with small gold mouldings. The execution seems thoroughly finished and excellent. . . .'

Pückler-Muskau's graphic description of this sumptuous room testifies to his minute

[1] Nash obtained Papal sanction to copy Raphael's arabesques in the Vatican. He sent Richard Evans to Rome to arrange the copying of these and other paintings. (Details in Shide Ledger).

[2] *See* Lytton: *Life of Edward Bulwer, 1st Lord Lytton.* (1913. Vol. I, p. 245.)

[3] Prince Pückler-Muskau, *op. cit.*, p. 231.

powers of observation unless he refreshed his memory with Britton and Pugin's *Public Buildings in London* published at this time in which there is an engraving. But he was wrongly informed about Nash having 'erected' an enormous fortune. He never did and what was more, his rewards for planning, designing and overseeing the West End improvements were meagre. His contract with the Commissioners of 1815 allowed a fee of £1,000 for all the work up to the end of 1814 with an additional sum of £2,500 for laying out the new sewer. After that he was paid 5 per cent on the cost of all public buildings, houses not yielding rent, ironwork, open spaces and lodges and for designs of a similar kind, but not executed, 1½ per cent of the estimated costs. For valuations, whether for purchase or sale, he received ¼ per cent, with 1¼ per cent on re-sales and more if the re-sale price exceeded the original by 10 per cent or more.[1] He was also expected to act as an estate agent for the Commissioners and if he let a site he received one half-year's rent which might amount to £10 or £20 on a first letting; and he was involved with the designing and supervising of the building, negotiating with builders and tenants and running each transaction as a separate and highly complicated enterprise. Thus the Commissioners had an architect, planner, interior decorator, surveyor and estate agent rolled into one. His responsibilities were enormous, his rewards few and his critics on every side.

We may therefore partly assume that Nash took it as his right to indulge himself extravagantly in East Cowes and in London. He may have seen that he would, on paper at any rate, always be in debt for no sooner did he recoup on one adventurous scheme than he plunged headlong into another. It was the nature of the man and, besides, the most spendthrift monarch in history was leading him on.

Before leaving the main-stream of the Regent Street developments and returning to London later only to witness Nash's fall over the building of Buckingham Palace, there are certain other West End developments which should not be overlooked.

Suffolk Street, a curious T-shaped quarter off the south-east end of the Haymarket, was a notoriously sinister meeting-place for frequenters of its brothels and dingy rooming-houses; its northern end was a dark cul-de-sac and to the south it led into what is now the eastern end of Pall Mall. This was obviously not a suitable little pocket of buildings to remain so close to the new improvements and in 1820 plans were laid to rebuild it. Nash persuaded his friend Edwards to invest in part of it, but later thought better of it; Nash is said to have bought Edwards's interest for £4,500 at his own valuation and we shall see that this transaction was to prove ominous. The façades of the development are varied and quite impressive although confined in a narrow street and most of them were designed by Nash. Several buildings survive, including part of the northern return into the Haymarket (where Nash's Llanayron-Southgate semi-circular tympana can be seen). The group

[1] Contract with Commissioners, 18th February, 1815. When examined by the Committee of 1828 Nash stated that he was remunerated for his work 'Very badly'.

represents the last surviving fragment of Nash's street architecture and is now known as Suffolk Place.

It was part of the improvements that Nash should allow for two theatres. One, the King's Opera House (designed by Nash and George Repton), occupied half the island site between the Haymarket and the lower part of Regent Street, with entrances in the Haymarket and the newly-forged Charles Street East. They encased the original theatre of 1790 in a splendid colonnaded shell, including shops and offices with Nash's attractive Royal Opera Arcade running behind.[1] The theatre was replaced by 'Her Majesty's' in 1893, but in spite of much rebuilding in the area, the arcade miraculously survives at the foot of towering New Zealand House of the 1960s.

Looking east from St James's Square across Regent Street and the Haymarket, the vista is stopped by the Theatre Royal, now known as the Haymarket Theatre. Finished in 1821 at the cost of £18,000[2] the great Corinthian portico still holds its own against later, less distinguished buildings and it is entirely due to Nash's enterprising negotiations that the old existing theatre site was moved south so that the new building should be so well placed. The interior, since much altered, must have had a rich and exotic atmosphere with its gold decorations on crimson and purple backgrounds, proscenium flanked by gilded palm-trees and flickering gas-lights.

The last and very important piece of town-planning was started in 1827 and it was to mean that the houses in the newly-fashionable Waterloo Place would no longer be in the hallowed precincts of the royal palace. The Prince had long tired of Carlton House, with its low ceilings and unpalatial air, even though Holland had enlarged and altered it and Nash had devised some sumptuous decorations.[3] As we shall see, Buckingham House, at the western end of the Mall, was to become the new palace and while plans were being laid for this, additional revenue was required. With Carlton House out of the way, Nash was commissioned to fill the site with rent-yielding properties and in 1827 Carlton House Terrace and Gardens were begun. Heroic in scale the twin blocks of houses stand terraced above the Mall divided by the entrance to Waterloo Place and facing south over St James's Park. The feeble pediments in the centre of each block add nothing to a fulsome display of giant Corinthian columns that run the whole length of the stucco façades without a break. The attic floor is set back behind a balustrated cornice and the end blocks of five bays are raised a storey higher to flank it. The composition is in the Regent's Park tradition[4] containing elements of several of the terraces, but the houses are much larger and the first

[1] There are excellent drawings at the R.I.B.A.

[2] Britton and Pugin: Vol. 1, pp. 262–72.

[3] Described and illustrated in W. H. Pyne: *Royal Residences*, 1819. Nash's work consisted of remodelling the basement to form a suite of Classical and Gothic rooms.

[4] Sir John Summerson notes that the terraces owe something to Nash's visits to Paris and reflect Gabriel's twin palaces in the Place de la Concorde. See *Georgian London*, 1945, p. 171.

48. Cornwall Terrace, 1820: a Corinthian block terminating in a caryatid-decorated bow window; from a drawing in the Crace Collection, British Museum.

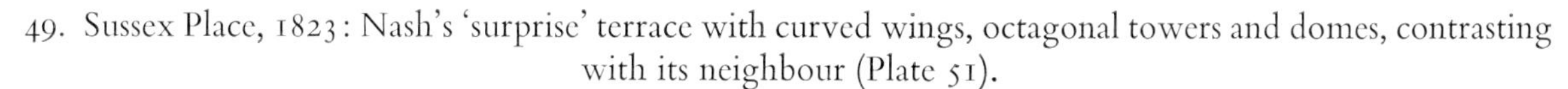

49. Sussex Place, 1823: Nash's 'surprise' terrace with curved wings, octagonal towers and domes, contrasting with its neighbour (Plate 51).

50. Park Village East, from 1825: the Park Villages provided picturesque scenery on either side of the Regent's Canal east of the Park (Elmes).

51. The Roman Doric Hanover Terrace of 1822 (Elmes).

52. Gloucester Gate, 1827: an Ionic block of large houses, the last to be completed in the Park.

53. Cumberland Terrace, 1826: this was Nash's great theatrical panorama. The blocks are linked by arches behind which are pairs of smaller houses (Elmes).

57. Regent Street: Soane's design on the east side, north of Beak Street (Elmes).

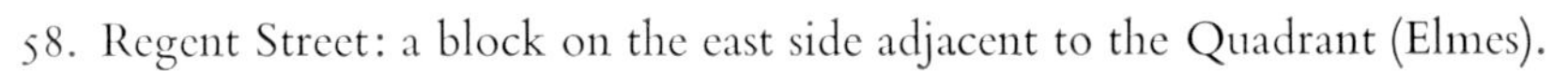
58. Regent Street: a block on the east side adjacent to the Quadrant (Elmes).

59. Regent Street: a block with Ionic and Doric features on the west side (Elmes).

60. Regent Street: a Corinthian block on the east side (Elmes).

61. Regent Street: west side (Elmes).

62. Regent Street: the west side of Regent Street from the Quadrant with the Vigo Street corner on the left (Elmes).

tenants were drawn from the ranks of the rich aristocracy.[1] Adjacent to the terraces other large houses formed Carlton Gardens,[2] all except one detached pair having given way to a modern block of flats and offices. At this time Nash was also laying out and replanting St James's Park in Reptonian style, which would later enhance the landscape towards Westminster and the eastern prospect from Buckingham Palace.

It might be thought that when Nash became involved with the Regent's metropolitan improvements he devoted all his energy to planning, designing, negotiating and supervising these gigantic schemes; but that is far from the case. As an architect to the Commissioners he was responsible for the day-to-day work involved with the Crown estates in London, Windsor and elsewhere, including alterations to the palaces of St James's, Kensington and Hampton Court.

1814 saw Nash designing temporary buildings at Carlton House and in St James's Park for the peace celebrations of that year. Napoleon's defeat was also celebrated with a grand reception for Wellington, later to become Nash's antagonist, and the architect devised several splendid rooms for this occasion in the gardens of Carlton House. In August of the same year he designed a bridge over the ornamental canal in the park surmounted by a pagoda[3] for yet another celebration—that of the centenary of the accession of George I. The year following the approval of the improvements he was commissioned to turn a small cottage in Windsor Great Park into a country retreat for the Prince. Known as the King's Cottage (1812–14) in later years and subsequently to be rebuilt to form the Royal Lodge of today, it was Nash's largest essay in picturesque cottage style, a development of the Blaise Hamlet group. But it was no mere cottage in spite of its thatched roof, gables and the other 'Old-English' details. The interior was spacious; a large service wing was concealed behind shrubbery and the rooms were fitted up in lavish style. At one time it was said that £200,000 was spent on the property[4] and if this were true, the Treasury would have remembered with dismay Nash's first estimate of about £14,000. It was contemptuously referred to as the Prince's 'Thatched Palace'.[5]

It was at this time, when the Cottage was building, that things started to get out of hand financially; it was the Treasury's first real taste of what was to come. Had Nash concentrated

[1] Nash's original sketch plans and architect's certificates for Sir Matthew White Ridley's house (No 10), are in the possession of Viscount Ridley.

[2] At this time Nash was also building the United Service Club on the corner of Pall Mall and Waterloo Place, originally part of the Carlton House land. The story of why this building does not match Decimus Burton's Athenaeum Club on the opposite corner of Pall Mall is told by John Cornforth: *Country Life*, April 12th, 1962. A plan in the library at Windsor Castle (Red Portfolio), recently discovered by Miss Dorothy Stroud, shows an earlier design for the Waterloo Place–Carlton House Terrace scheme.

[3] The pagoda, illuminated at night, caught fire and fell into the canal; the bridge and the stump of the pagoda survived for many years. There are illustrations in Papworth: *Select Views*, 1816. *See* also Neville Braybrooke: *London Green*, 1959, p. 183.

[4] *See* T. E. Harwood: *Windsor Old and New*, 1929.

[5] *Roger Fulford: George IV*, 1949, p. 123.

only on schemes approved by the Commissioners and the Treasury he would, no doubt, have ended his days as a revered State architect. He would have had in common with all prominent architects the usual frustrating and tedious financial dealings with the Government and censure from envious rivals and amateur critics; but Nash was equal to all this. Instead he preferred the more adventurous dual *rôle* of architect to the Commissioners of Crown Lands and personal architect to the Prince. What Nash sadly misjudged was the ever-increasing unpopularity of the Prince and there is little to show that the latter amassed his great collections of pictures and furniture, and buildings in which to display them, for any other reason than to satisfy his own vanity. It is difficult to justify his greed for such things on the grounds that his foremost desire was to enrich the Crown or the artistic heritage of the country, although in satisfying his whims and gratifying his tastes he did both. His private life was notoriously squalid and his personal debts mounted until they became matters of national concern. By the time he was in trouble over the building of Buckingham Palace, his gross indulgences had rendered him a monster quite without power to save the architect of his extravagances. To a man of Nash's background and temperament it would have been impossible for him to resist either the Commissioners or the Prince and in any case, both masters were controlled by the same bank—the Treasury.

CHAPTER SIX

The Oriental Vision

THE only major work that Nash carried out for the Prince without the initial necessity of Treasury sanction was the Royal Pavilion at Brighton and although Nash probably visited Brighton with Repton as early as 1797, he did not start to transform the existing building into its Oriental splendour until 1815; and it was not finished until 1823, only two years after the Prince had ascended the throne and two years before work at Buckingham Palace was to begin.

The Prince had first visited Brighton in 1783 at the age of twenty-one after the years of his youth had been spent under the hand of his stubborn, unyielding father, George III. He had attempted to put his mind to serious matters, but each of his suggestions was turned down until it was clear that the pursuit of pleasure was to be his only outlet. His uncle, the Duke of Cumberland, lived in Brighton and led a life of notorious licentiousness—the ideal Mecca for a young man bent on enjoying himself away from the restrictions of court life. Croly[1] tells us that at an even earlier date the Prince's future was sealed: 'At this stage the Prince was nineteen, as ripe an age as could be desired for ruin; and in three short years the consummation was arrived at—he was ruined.' His fresh, florid good looks and sartorial elegance made him an irresistible figure of admiration and flattery and he very soon became the spoiled, adored leader of the sycophantic society that flocked to Brighton in his wake.

Brighton was then a small fashionable spa with a holiday air and the Prince was to make it his favourite playground and the Pavilion his most treasured toy; it was to become the scene of his great romance with Mrs Fitzherbert and other amorous escapades and the setting for much magnificent entertaining.

The first 'pavilion' was a Classical villa by Henry Holland, and the central feature of the

[1] George Croly: *Personal History of George IV*, 1841.

plan was a circular drawing room with semi-circular apses, communicating on each side with pairs of other reception rooms. The main elevation showed a domed Ionic peristyle containing the round room flanked by wings with shallow bow windows; altogether a pleasing façade of country house appearance. The villa was built in five months; Nash's final designs were the result of thirty-five years of metamorphosis; but Holland's plan remained the nucleus of all later alterations.[1]

In 1805 Repton had fired the Prince's imagination with designs for a new pavilion in Indian taste, inspired by his visits to Sezincote, Gloucestershire, where C. R. Cockerell had built a country house in Hindu style. The Prince was delighted by their originality and promised that 'not a tittle shall be altered—even you yourself shall not admit any improvement'.[2] But Repton's ambitions were doomed; the scheme was ill-timed and money for such an elaborate building was short at Carlton House. The matter was shelved and it was Nash who, twelve years later, was to produce the real vision of the East. Repton was paid £715 13s. 6d. for his designs, poor compensation for seeing his erstwhile partner carry out the work and for which he was paid ten times that amount. On 9th June, 1814, Repton described with disgust in a disjointed letter[3] how he lost the pavilion work to Nash in 1808:

> . . . H.R.H. after expressing the most perfect satisfaction with all I propose—put it into the hands of the Surveyor General—because he could do it at the public expense and I was of course superseded—and since his death—he has appointed Nash to be Surveyor general which I had the fullest reason to expect from his having mentioned him with contempt and his warm economiums of all I have proposed at Brighton—when my hopes of future eminence were blown like an empty bladder—or the bubble of a Child—And after seeing the only man on earth with whom I had ever quarrelled raised to the situation to which I had reasonably aspired—I can only say—Cursed is the man who puts his trust in princes—and so ended my royal hopes. . . .

James Wyatt was George III's favourite architect and as Surveyor-General and Comptroller of the Board of Works, would have been responsible for any work carried out at Brighton; but his death in a carriage accident in 1813 gave the Prince his long-awaited opportunity to replace him with Nash, who was duly appointed over the august heads of Smirke and Soane, more likely candidates, thus nurturing the seeds of antagonism between Nash and the latter that had existed since the 1790s. Nash was appointed Deputy Surveyor-General and later he became an 'Attached Architect' to the Office of Works with Soane and Smirke, each architect being responsible for a separate part of public developments.

[1] For illustrations and story of the transformation see Clifford Musgrave: *Royal Pavilion—an Episode in the Romantic*, 2nd ed., 1959.

[2] Loudon, *op. cit.*, p. 19.

[3] To Sir H. Fetherstonhaugh of Uppark where Repton and Nash worked. *See* M. Meade-Fetherstonhaugh and O. Warner: *Uppark and its People*, 1964, pp. 72–73.

William Porden's royal stables had been built in 1803 and these were in 'correct' Indian style—the first buildings of exotic character to appear on the Pavilion estate. Nash's contribution to the scheme was to be altogether different in feeling: Porden's sombre buildings were, indeed, Indian, but touches of gaiety, lightness and fantasy were quite absent.

On plan, Nash added two great rooms to Holland's villa (already remodelled in 1801–03 by P. F. Robinson, Holland's nephew)—a banqueting room to the south and a music room to the north. The original reception rooms flanking the central dome had already been opened up to form larger rooms and now all five rooms were inter-communicating, facing east over the gardens. The west front was not bound by Holland's shell and was built out to include two entrance vestibules, the royal bedroom, library, guest suites and a long gallery or corridor. Hidden away behind shrubbery in the usual manner were the vast kitchen and servants' quarters to the south.

The construction of the exterior decorations (for such they may be called) was a long and laborious procedure. Basically it went as follows: The two new rooms at each end were box-like in shape and were given tent-like domes; at each corner of the boxes rose minarets to the height of the domes and each wall was pierced by five Indian–Gothic windows. Over each of Holland's humble bows, linking the new rooms to the central feature, grew onion domes topped with finials; but the main feature was the gigantic central onion dome sitting above Holland's old drawing room and closely flanked by minarets. Thus the main silhouette was achieved and an arched verandah of fretted stone, with Indian style crenellations along the parapets, supplied the necessary unifying elements. This description simplifies the composition to a degree, but it is the principle on which the remodelling was based and Nash's brilliant use of rich and elaborate detail combined to give the exterior its dazzling appearance.

So extravagant are the decorations of the main rooms that they defy detailed description and were not, in any case, entirely devised by Nash. The gallery, gained through an immense domed *porte-cochère* and the two vestibules, was decorated in pink with delicate blue Chinese motifs of bamboo, trees and rocks. Twin cast-iron double-return staircases at each end of the room had balusters of simulated bamboo and risers of finely-pierced brass. This was a pretty room and beautifully executed, but the Chinese style in itself was not a new idea: Chinese wallpaper had been presented to the Prince in 1802[1] and used in the old rooms; Porden had proposed a Chinese exterior for the Pavilion in 1805;[2] ceramics from the East and furniture influenced by Oriental designs had become increasingly popular since the mid-18th century.

The great banqueting room, rising to the height of the southern tent dome, was an entirely different matter. Here there was no question of using the Chinese style alone and

[1] *See* E. W. Brayley: *Her Majesty's Palace at Brighton*, 1838.

[2] There is a watercolour drawing of his design at the Royal Pavilion exhibited at the Royal Academy of that year.

all the motifs of the East are assembled and used in a way never before seen. The basic shape of the room was Classical with coves and spandrels, but this was disguised under a profusion of multi-coloured decorations giving an effect of unparalleled richness. The central dome was filled with massive plantain leaves, some painted directly on to the ceiling, others free-standing, from which hung a silver and green dragon in turn supporting an immense chandelier of crystal; lights in the form of lotus flowers were held in the mouths of more dragons. From four pendants smaller chandeliers hung from the necks of exotic gilded birds. The wall surfaces were decorated with panels of Chinese figures and any other remaining wall-space was painted in arabesques of dragons' tails, or richly gilded and latticed. Curious lozenge-shaped windows filled the eastern and western spandrels and those facing the gardens were heavily draped in crimson silk. The room does not stand up to analysis and was never intended to do so, but the total effect was one of exotic magnificence and this was its aim.

In contrast the two rooms to the north and south of the round saloon were notably restrained. Because they retained Holland's old ceiling-heights the proportions of the rooms were on a more domestic scale and they contained Chinese decorations of a rich but unflamboyant nature. These rooms had been decorated and redecorated several times before and their final appearance coincided with Nash's two great rooms. The saloon, that bastion and core of the original villa, was also again transformed and, although the pier-glasses, wall-panels and pelmets had crestings in Indian style, it took on the appearance of a more conventional drawing room of the period, richly decorated in crimson, white and gold and with a crystal chandelier suspended from a circular dome painted to resemble the sky.

The music room was another sumptuous extravaganza and, if it can be compared at all, more grotesque and perhaps less impressive than the banqueting room. The general impression of colour given by the decorations was of orange-red and gold offset by the blue in the curtains and carpet. The massive wall-paintings depicted Chinese scenes conjuring up romantic visions of the East and were flanked by painted columns entwined with serpents; fire-breathing dragons filled the top corners of the scenes. The great dome was decorated with gilded diminishing scallop shells—an 'Oriental' version of traditional diminishing coffering used in Classical design. The immense chandelier of painted glass was shaped like a water-lily and surrounded by eight smaller versions. The organ, occupying the centre of the north wall, was set under a coved ceiling of bamboo strips repeated at the opposite end of the room.

These two great rooms have no precedent in the Western World (or indeed in the Eastern) and may have been inspired by Marco Polo's descriptions of Oriental palaces.[1] Elegance was not the object but to evoke the fairy-tale land of the East was—with all its mysteries and enchantment combined into fantastic schemes of decoration.

[1] Musgrave: *op. cit.*, p. 108.

While the rooms were being devised (mostly by Frederick Crace[1] under Nash's wing) much furniture in Oriental style was being specially designed by Robert Jones and made by Bailey and Saunders. Furniture came and went; fireplaces were transported from other royal residences and fittings were moved from place to place. At no time was the Pavilion really static in appearance, but the best picture of it showing the rooms as Nash left them is to be seen in a volume of aquatints and engravings produced by him at the command of his royal patron. The title page of a prospectus of 1824 reads:

SHORTLY WILL BE PUBLISHED
BY THE COMMAND OF, AND DEDICATED BY PERMISSION TO
HIS MOST GRACIOUS MAJESTY
Views and Illustrations
OF
HIS MAJESTY'S PALACE
AT
BRIGHTON
BY JOHN NASH, ESQ.
PRIVATE ARCHITECT TO THE KING
Etc. Etc. Etc.

The volume was bound in purple morocco, sold at twenty guineas and the plates were destroyed after 250 copies had been printed. Augustus Pugin, by this time a most accomplished and distinguished draughtsman, made original water-colour drawings from which the aquatints were made and these, extremely beautiful in themselves, are now preserved at the Pavilion.

The middle of the century saw the decline in the fortunes of the Pavilion. William IV liked the place and was seen there with Nash, then seventy-eight, shortly after his accession;[2] but Queen Victoria found its lack of privacy in a small seaside town intolerable and the aesthetic dream of exotic palaces was not hers. She decided to give up the Pavilion as a royal residence and remove most of the furniture and furnishings. In 1847 a sale was held to dispose of the remaining furniture and certain pieces passed into private hands. The building was now an empty shell; there were thoughts of demolishing it and developing the site. After protracted local discussions and difficult negotiations with the Commissioners of Woods and Forests, the estate was finally bought by the Brighton Town Commissioners in 1850 for £53,000. It had cost over £500,000 to create.

[1] Son of John Crace, head of the firm who supplied most of the designs and decorations for the rooms. They also supplied furniture and furnishings imported from China. Frederick Crace presented his great collection of maps, drawings and prints of London to the British Museum.

[2] *See* p. 100.

A year later the Office of the Woods and Forests desecrated the interior, ruthlessly tearing down wall decorations and damaging the fabric and floors. The ceilings were, however, left intact and the Town Commissioners began the task of restoring the rooms sufficiently for the building to be used for civic receptions, exhibitions and other functions —a rôle that it fulfills to this day. In 1864 the Queen returned many of the original fittings, still unpacked, under the enlightened influence of Francis Edmund De Val, the first Custodian of the Pavilion. This gesture was the first of several made by the Royal Family in ensuing years and many pieces of furniture have since been restored to their original positions.

Dark, late-Victorian and Edwardian decorations obscured the Pavilion's true character for many years, but the slow, painstaking task of proper restoration followed and today, under the meticulous hand of Mr Clifford Musgrave, Director of the Pavilion since 1945, visitors can once again marvel at this masterpiece of architectural whimsy.

Not all Nash's dealings with the Prince (who became George IV in 1820 during the most important part of the building) were tranquil. The King had ruled as Regent for nine years during his father's madness and by the time things had progressed far with the Pavilion schemes, his finances had become bound up with those of the State;[1] so what started as a private toy became the subject of public expenditure. In 1821 Nash was having a disagreeable correspondence[2] with Sir Benjamin Bloomfield (the King's private secretary and, in fact, well-disposed to Nash), and it told the usual story of over-spending. The cost of the building had, of course, been very high, but in justice to Nash the work was extremely complicated and the King's demands extravagant; all new excesses were carried out and it is small wonder that estimates were exceeded.[3] The King's moods were, in any case, always dictated by his freedom (or lack of it) to spend money and by the success (or otherwise) of his amorous caprices. Until his final break with Mrs Fitzherbert in 1811 his private life had been reasonably ordered for some years, but by the time of his quarrel with Nash he was hopelessly dissolute; although nothing remained of his good looks, his sexual vanity, unlike his financial resources, knew no limits. Frustration in either of these fundaments would lead to trouble and Nash, ever-ready to do his master's bidding, added fuel to financial chaos. In order to try and help matters, Nash offered to forego his commissions of £7,800, but eventually matters were resolved to everyone's satisfaction.[4]

The King spent Christmas of 1824 at the Pavilion; he was prevented by illness from further visits until January, 1827, when he visited the place for the last time, bringing with him 'four grand pianofortes' for his entertainment.[5]

[1] In 1815 the Prince had channelled all building costs at the Pavilion to the Privy Purse.

[2] Windsor Archives, George IV Accounts, Res. and Prop., Brighton Pavilion.

[3] Complete accounts for the Pavilion are in the Windsor Archives.

[4] Summerson: *op. cit.*, footnote 1, p. 166.

[5] Information of Mr Musgrave.

63. 14–16, Regent Street: Nash's gallery which was dismantled and completely reconstructed at East Cowes Castle on his retirement. Lawrence used this room as a background to his portrait of Nash (*See* frontispiece); an engraving from J. Britton and A. Pugin: *Illustrations of the Public Buildings of London* 1825–27.

64. Suffolk Place, Haymarket, 1820–23: a fragment of surviving street architecture belonging to the West End developments.

73. The Royal Pavilion: the Banqueting Room.

74. The Music Room: although Nash inspired the sumptuous decorations, various designers and craftsmen worked under the personal supervision of the Prince Regent.

CHAPTER SEVEN

Ill-timed Splendour

HAVING turned the Pavilion into a palace, Nash was now commanded to do the same for Buckingham House, which George III had presented to his wife and therefore was sometimes known as the 'Queen's House'. But before we follow the history of this ill-fated undertaking, we should consider Nash's position as a figure on the professional scene of the day.

Ever since his scheme for the London improvements was accepted he had become a public figure; no longer the successful architect content to design houses for the rich and accept a few interesting commissions from public bodies and the Government, as were his rivals, but a man who had willed himself to be *the* architect of the day, by talent, relentless drive and boundless optimism. His success brought enemies, not only because of the dubious methods he employed to attain his position, but also because jealousy, envy and spite so often accompany fame; and Nash's fame at that time was largely due to the patronage of an extravagant monarch. It could have happened to any other candidate, but there was none; and no other monarch had dared to reshape the face of London. Had the King been thrifty, discreet and well-respected, Nash would not have been his man, nor would Regent Street have been built. They were victims of each other's ambitions and it was Nash who paid the final price. His downfall was to coincide with Parliament's exasperation at the King's extravagances and, even if the building of Buckingham Palace had been a successful venture, the architect's days were numbered with those of his patron. Everyone was tired of the endless expenditure and the antagonism was cumulative.

Nash was lampooned and ridiculed on all sides in the crude and boisterous manner of the day, but so were other people in the public eye, and when a cartoon showed the architect impaled on the steeple of his much-ridiculed All Souls's Church,[1] he is said to have

[1] *See* A. T. Bolton: *op. cit.*

commented 'See, gentlemen, how criticism has exalted me'. His relationship with Soane—who bitterly resented the King's favouritism of Nash, but was utterly unsuited by temperament to take his place had it been offered—was one of good-humoured chiding on Nash's part, and neurotic, rather pathetic, forbearance on Soane's. Unlike Nash, Soane had painfully evolved his own peculiar brand of late Neo-Classicism with its morbid preoccupation with urns, sarcophagi, antefixae and incised pilasters. His work was distinguished, original and serious, but he had not Nash's vision for planning or his thrusting personality. Soane was a tortured and introverted character with a strongly marked persecution complex; Nash was strongly extroverted and, as so often happens, a source of irritation to those of quieter disposition. Soane was knighted in 1831 and, although he had a most distinguished career, he had to see real fame and royal patronage being enjoyed by one whose work was greatly inferior to his own. He was constantly being fed with gossiping letters from Spiller and Burdon about Nash's conduct. In 1822 Burdon wrote to Soane:[1] 'I hear miserable accounts of that . . . Nash's proceedings. Has no one the boldness, I had almost said honesty, to inform his master of his real character? . . .'

Because of his elevated position in architectural circles, Nash's relationships with other architects were bound to be unrealistic and influenced by professional tensions and jealousies. He had made an enemy of Repton (but retained the loyalty of his son George); he had made other enemies, politically and socially, but it is almost impossible to distinguish estrangements from quarrels, envy from mere criticism, at such long distance without more evidence; one must rely on documents which, often isolated from their true context, can only show a small part of the picture. A letter[2] from Nash to Soane at the time when the latter had been ordered to hand over the drawings of Buckingham Palace to the former does, however, provide us with a brilliantly illuminating glimpse of Nash's character and bears reprinting:

East Cowes Castle, Isle of Wight,
September 18, 1822.

Brother Soane,

You was in a miff when I saw you at the head of Your Masons. One of the Masonic rules, I am told, is to acquire a meek and humble spirit. I fear therefore You are not qualified for Grand Master. Now, if You will but come here and copy me for a month, You will certainly be appointed to a higher niche in Your Lodge when You next meet, and see poor Bloomfield with kinder aspect than You were wont to do, and do penance for the hard thoughts You expressed of him. He is as innocent of the crime You imputed to him, as You are of *any* crime—but, my dear Soane, I did not mean to sermonize when I sat down to address You, but to say that I cannot come up as soon as Sunday and therefore thought it due to You to give You the earliest notice, and absolve You from

[1] *Ibid.*

[2] *Ibid.*

the appointment for Monday, which You were so kind as to accede to. The Churches must therefore be without our architectural consecration till we meet, unless You and your colleagues will perform the ceremony, and which I much wish You would do, as I am anxious the trowel shall be used on one of them [St George's] before the winter sets in, which I smell every morning about 6 o'clock, an hour which I suppose finds you . . . (in bed).

When I left You—musing upon Your wild-goose chase of Bloomfield— it occurred to me that our appointments are perfectly Constitutional, I, the King, You, the Lords, and *Your* friend Smirke, the Commons, and the blood instantly rushed to my face seeing, or fancying, that You wanted to dethrone me. It then struck me that You wanted to be both King and Lords, and in fancy I heard You cry out 'Off with his head, so much for *Buckingham*,' and I sighed 'why should he so long for my empty chair when a few years would give him that without offense which has occasioned in him so offensive an act,' for I am old, but feeling my head on my shoulders I marched off to Buckingham House. I had not gone 6 steps before I was stopped by the *Black Rod*, he demanded whether the south aperture of the arcade was to be stop'd up. I took him by the arm and pointing my finger said 'Lo !, the architect of the fabrick,' and would have ushered him into the presence; 'shall I *usher* you,' said I, but, whether the term smelt too much of the shop, or he thought I meant to insult him, I know not, but off he marched. I recollected myself and had a quarm, I beg your pardon, I mean qualm something too much of this.

I have scribbled so much that I am in doubt when next we meet You will wear a face 'most in grief or anger—'. I hope neither, but lighted up by smiles, not such smiles as would seem 'to scorn Your spirit that would be moved to smile at anything', but the smile of cordiality which, be assured, I feel for you, or, if you strain a point and present Yourself at our drawbridge, I shall believe you actuated with the same spirit, and, till you do so, the sumptuous dinner You gave my trio at your elegant, doublefaced mansion will not sit quite easy on my stomach. The portcullis will rise at the touch of Your masterly finger and the master spring to give you welcome.

With you dear Soane,
I've picked a bone,
And fain I would requite it;
Should you refuse,
I cannot choose,
Ah! let me not indite it.
But fist or stick,
A bone must pick
With you and out must fight it.

Very bad! very bad! Off! Off! Well I am off, but one word more at parting, Mrs Nash and the 'Sweet Ann Page' desire me to say that they will expect you, and believe me I often think of You. As a proof, I have Your figure before my eyes, a thin black shadow standing on the foundation walls of the new arcade, with arms folded contemplating the mode of laying bricks. Oh that I had leisure for such contemplation, and that some friend could describe my thick, squat, dwarf figure, with round head, snub nose, and little eyes, in such an act of contemplation; but I must be shot *flying*. All joking being at an end with my paper (luckily for you), I conclude in sober sadness a l'ordinaire, but with truth not appertaining to the custom, that I am, My dear Soane,

Very Sincerely Yours
John Nash.

J. Soane, Esq., Architect to the whole Peerage of England.

Here is all the stuff of grand histrionics, facetiousness and bombast, calculated to make it quite clear who was master (and why) and to tease a rival lacking the resilience to take the ups and downs of life in a spirit of good humour. Soane's reply[1] is shorter and reveals the austerity of his nature and his inability to realise that Nash was never much worried by criticism or even failure:

13 Lincoln's Inn Fields, London.
Sept. 24, 1822.

Many thanks, my dear Sir, for Your very kind serio-comic Epistle. Be assured I have long since known that 'Seneca is not too serious nor Plautus too light' for Your prolific brain. I will endeavour to follow Your advice and tread in Your steps, and although I cannot, at this time, quit business and enjoy the festivities and hospitality of East Cowes Castle, I will strive to fancy myself at least of your party. You, my dear friend, may smile at my attention to professional pursuits, but I am convinced there are few persons more anxious of fame, and who would make greater sacrifices at the shrine of public approbation, than yourself.

Fame you possess, and you also have a friend who if ever the bitter shaft of envy or malice should reach You, that friend would kiss away the falling tear and smooth the pillow of sadness.

Again let me offer my best thanks for Your kind and friendly invitation to Cowes, and with sincere wishes for the health, happiness and prosperity of Mrs Nash and Yourself, believe me, with sentiments of regard, My Dear Sir,

Very truly Yours
John Soane.

[1] *Ibid.*

We know little of Nash's relationships with other prominent colleagues (though he is known to have actively disliked Smirke) yet doubtless they were dismayed that the lion's share of work came through the back door of Carlton House. But there must have been colleagues on humbler levels who were Nash's loyal friends and many others who profited by their contributions to his schemes; it is significant, too, that when Nash was later on trial for alleged professional misconduct no-one who knew him well or had worked with him showed evidence of personal animosity.

When Buckingham Palace was begun in 1825 Nash's life was certainly one of complex pressures and during the next few years these were to become hopelessly out of control. To follow the crowded sequence of events that resulted in this, we must first remember that Nash's triumph over Soane with regard to the Palace designs was, in fact, no triumph at all. Even allowing for the financial chaos that was to ensue, Nash's position and reputation might have been saved if his designs had been good; but they were not and things went from bad to worse.

No English monarch had ever possessed a great London palace; St James's Palace was a miniature Hampton Court and Carlton House merely a much-disguised early-Georgian mansion, and both were little more than large country-houses in town; Whitehall had long been abandoned as a royal residence. Buckingham Palace was to be different—the answer to the great town palaces on the Continent; something to show that the Monarchy was housed in splendid style in a newly-grand capital. But it was too late and a new, prosaic outlook was emerging. The Monarchy and its advisers were soon to realise the prudence of building and living more moderately, although, in justice to Nash, enormous sums were soon to be spent on additions and alterations to the Palace, few of which had anything to do with his original work. Yet the King was determined and Nash was in no position to refuse further commands.

Four years were to pass between Soane handing over his Palace plans[1] and Nash preparing new ones, during which time the latter was still working at the Pavilion, decorating state rooms at St James's Palace, designing a royal stand at Ascot, building Clarence House[2] and, of course, continually busy with the Regent Street–Mall developments. He was seventy-three when he started on the Palace and it seems clear that his powers were failing. The drawings were prepared in a hurry with apparently little attention paid to co-ordinated planning or design.[3] Originally the King had suggested that the new building

[1] A watercolour drawing by Gandy at Sir John Soane's Museum shows Soane's splendid and dramatic design for the Palace.

[2] Adjacent to St James's Palace, 1825; for the Duke of Clarence, later William IV. Nash's original elevation to the Mall has largely disappeared under alterations and additions from 1873.

[3] *See* Christopher Hussey's introduction to H. Clifford Smith: *The Complete History of Buckingham Palace*, p. 39. The first plans and designs for the Palace have not survived. Drawings of some of the later (1827–28) alterations are in the Victoria and Albert Museum.

should be *pied-à-terre*[1] on the site of old Buckingham House[2] but, as always, what started as a modest idea, like the Pavilion and the King's Cottage, soon became an uncontrollable monster.

An engraving from a drawing by Pugin shows the original east front which incorporated some of the fabric of the old house and, although some of the individual features were original and lively, such as the lofty terminal pavilions of the flanking wings and the square, isolated attic windows (all elements from Nash's 'long-distant' vocabulary), the composition was a failure. It was eccentric without being distinguished; the architect had lost his touch and even though it is vastly more interesting than what exists today, this elevation was a perfect target for ridicule. The garden front was more successful[3] and the small dome which looked absurd from the east peeping over the central pediment, formed a proper part of the composition surmounting the semi-circular Corinthian bay in the centre.[4] As the building progressed it became increasingly obvious that the parts failed to form any sort of unity.

Financing the building was little short of a hoax by the King and Nash who were determined to do exactly what they wanted. Work was in progress before the Bill had passed the House of Commons authorising a sum that 'might not be less than £200,000' for the 'repair and improvement' of Buckingham House. In other words, the Government probably imagined that the old house would be modernised and improved for the King as a suitable substitute for Carlton House.[5] Before long an entirely new building was emerging and by 1828 not only had the original estimate been made to seem absurd, but Nash's most devastating enemy appeared—Wellington, the new Prime Minister. Nash went to see him about the Palace early that year[6] and suggested that the wings should, at the King's request, be demolished and rebuilt. But the Duke, who had no intention of getting himself identified with the extravagances of the King, commented sharply: 'If you expect me to put my hand to any additional expense, I'll be damned if I will!' By now the King was seriously ailing and the Duke could see that it would probably not be long before the scene would change and he would no longer be obliged to consider his whims. In any case Wellington was not a man to be influenced by anything other than his own conscience.

[1] *See* Summerson: *op. cit.* p. 234.

[2] Built for John Sheffield, 1703, Duke of Buckingham, by William Winde. It contained a grand staircase hall with frescoes by Laguerre. *See* illustration in Clifford Smith: *op. cit.*

[3] Although much altered by subsequent architects, the fabric of the garden (west) front is still substantially Nash's. Blore, and later Pennethorne, incorporated Nash's work in additions and alterations. The existing State Ballroom and State Supper room block at the south end of the Palace of 1854 is by Pennethorne.

[4] Sir Albert Richardson noted that the general style of the Palace designs were French-influenced. *See* also Clifford Smith: *op. cit.*, p. 41.

[5] Nash had earlier proposed the rebuilding of Carlton House. Two oil-paintings of alternative designs—Classical and Gothic—are at Buckingham Palace and are reproduced in Clifford Smith: *op. cit.*

[6] *The Creevey Papers*, 1905, p. 498.

As one of the 'Attached Architects' Nash was entitled to a remuneration of 3 per cent, but he obtained sanction from the King and the Treasury to have this increased to 5 per cent to cover the expenses of paying his draughtsmen; the increase was granted providing he laid no claim to his retaining salary of £500.[1] But the initial clouds of Government disapproval were now descending on Nash for his unorthodox methods of making contracts with the various tradesmen.

Nash's instructions were to get prices for materials and labour from individual tradesmen and to proceed with the work after approval of the Treasury; or, failing to obtain approval after so many days, to proceed without it. The tradesmen were to agree to provide their services at a certain percentage below a standard rate fixed by the Board of Works who later measured the work and paid the tradesmen.[2] Nash, however, disapproved of this method and preferred contracts to be in gross, each tradesman contracting to do the whole amount of work required for an agreed sum. He affirmed that a uniform reduction of 10 per cent (which he had arranged in all trades) was more satisfactory and that in this way he was able to obtain better workmanship and not merely the cheapest; here Nash was out of bounds and although the King did not care in the least how the financial side was managed, the new Government did.

Almost as soon as the Government was in power, a member of the Opposition in the House of Commons moved for a committee to enquire into the expense of public buildings. Nash, Soane, Smirke, Wyatville, and others appeared before a Select Committee and the examination started on March 25th, 1828. On April 3rd Nash was on trial and the question of Buckingham Palace was raised thus marking the most ominous moment in his life. It was the first of a series of Select Committees that were to blight the remainder of his career.

The findings make poignant and pathetic reading. At the cost of £50,000 the offending wings of the Palace had been raised to the height of the main block and elaborate Corinthian porticos added to match the existing one in the centre. The whole building was faced with Bath stone, greatly more expensive than stucco and, to add to the cost (and the confusion of ideas), a marble arch was placed between the wings, contrasting oddly with its background. The arch, removed to the junction of Oxford Street and Park Lane in 1847, was built of Ravaccione marble especially imported from Italy and the sculpture was executed by Westmacott, Baily and Chantrey.[3] At the Committee Nash admitted that the wings of the Palace were a blunder and he tried to justify the existence of the unfortunate dome as follows:

[1] All three 'Attached Architects' received a £500 retaining salary.

[2] 1831, Select Committee, report on, App. 111, 1. p. 194.

[3] Details of the transaction are in the report of the 1831 Select Committee.

Is any light conveyed from the top of the dome?
None at all.

Then it is purely an ornamental part of the building?
It forms the ceiling of the room underneath.
That is not one of the state rooms?
No, it is over one of the state rooms.

But the inquisitors were still in the dark.

Will you inform the committee whether any useful part of the building is lighted by means of the dome.
There is no light from the dome, but the cavity of the dome is necessary to make the room underneath the dome of a proper height.
Is it a room of great utility?
No, nothing but a common bedroom.

However, in the midst of all censure Nash was serving his master well. He had designed a series of state rooms for the Palace that had never been equalled in grandeur and the King was delighted. Although these great rooms were created during Nash's downfall (some to be modified by Blore and later by others) they still exist today substantially as he designed them. In decoration Nash rarely went beyond fulsome Gothic or acceptable Classicism and the sweeping abandon of Baroque was completely out of his range; but in the Palace rooms we see 18th-century tradition stretched to the limit and they must represent the ultimate in Classical magnificence.

The Committee examined other of Nash's works besides the Palace; the questions being asked were ones of cost, authorization and merit of designs—executed or projected. What had not been queried was his personal integrity over business matters concerning his remuneration and dealings with Crown property until, by a strange twist of irony, a Colonel Davies, Member for Worcester (the town which held so many memories for Nash and his intimate circle at East Cowes), suddenly made a personal attack on his honesty concerning property deals in Suffolk Street and Regent's Park. This spiteful man appears to have had visions of rising to fame and acclaim on exposing 'the minion who has poured poison into the ear of the sovereign'[1] as he put it. But he was to be disappointed; Davies applied for a Select Committee to investigate the matter and after three weeks Nash was entirely exonerated on each charge. The Committee added, however, that it would be wiser for architects working in official capacities not to involve themselves with valuations of property in which they had an interest. Several friends rallied round to show their faith in the architect's integrity, but the proceedings did his tottering reputation no good. The

[1] *Hansard:* Vol. XXI (N.S.), p. 1578.

75. Buckingham Palace from 1825: the garden elevation as it appeared before alterations by Nash's successors. The pavilion on the right is now the Queen's Art Gallery; engraved from a drawing by T. Shepherd, 1831, in the London Museum.

76. Buckingham Palace: the east front before Nash rebuilt the side wings in an effort to improve the composition; engraved from a drawing by Pugin, 1827, in the London Museum.

77. Buckingham Palace: The Blue Drawing Room.

78. The White Drawing Room.

79. The Music Room. The decorations in this and other rooms in the Palace, although over-laid in some instances with later embellishments, are basically the work of Nash. The materials were ordered in 1825 and George IV expressed his delight with the schemes well before Nash's downfall.

Committee's findings spurred the King to rescue him from further attacks (which would reflect inevitably on himself) and he suggested to Wellington that a baronetcy should be conferred on the architect immediately:[1]

Royal Lodge, 14th June, 1829.

My Dear Friend,

I now write to you upon a matter in which I feel very *much* interested. The Report of the Committee of the House of Commons upon Mr Nash's business has been delivered in, and, as I am informed by one of that Committee (not one of those who had any previous predilection towards him) '*without the slightest stain or imputation upon or against his character,*' I do therefore desire that you will direct his being *gazetted by himself* on *Tuesday next, the 16th of this month*, as a Baronet, with the remainder at his death (as he, Nash, has no family of his own), to his nephew Mr Edwards, a gentleman of excellent character, large property, who sat in the last Parliament, and who has proved himself a thorough supporter of government, and a most *loyal man*, besides being well known to *me personally*. Mr Nash has been most infamously used, and there is but one opinion about it; and therefore it is not only an act of justice to *him* but to *my own dignity* that *this* should *forthwith* be *done*. For if those who go through the furnace for *me* and for *my service*, are not protected, the favour of the Sovereign *becomes worse than nugatory*

Your very sincere friend

G.R.

Wellington was not impressed with the idea, his reply stating that the Committee's findings had not yet been before the House. The Duke wrote to Mrs Arbuthnot:[2]

16th June 1829.

. . . I have a quarrel in hand with the King. He wished to make Nash a Baronet and to have him gazetted as on this day. I have objected on the ground, first that the Report of the Committee has not been made secondly that if the Report had been made, Mr Nash is employed on Buckingham House, and that it will not facilitate questions on that Palace if Mr Nash is created a Baronet before he will have passed his accounts . . .

and Mrs Arbuthnot noted in her journal on 26th:

H.M.'s present ill humour is caused by the Duke (WELLINGTON) refusing to make Mr Nash a baronet. The King says he is the only sovereign in Europe without power to confer an honour of this kind. The Duke says Mr Nash is in the public service, that his

[1] *Despatches & Memoranda of Field Marshal Arthur, Duke of Wellington*, 1880.

[2] *Wellington and his Friends*—letters of the 1st Duke selected and edited by the 7th Duke of Wellington, 1965.

conduct is under a course of enquiry before the House of Commons and that, while that is pending it is quite out of the question to prejudge the case and confer an honour upon Mr Nash that he has not the slightest doubt of Mr Nash's honesty, but that *now* was not the moment to grant him a favor from the Crown.

The timing was hopeless and almost exactly a year after he had written to Wellington the King died. He was not to see the Palace completed and by now the work itself was entirely out of control. The Government could now make even fuller enquiries into the reckless expenditure and Nash's career virtually ended with the death of his patron. In October of 1830 the Treasury suspended his commission and dismissed him from the Board of Works; all work on the Palace was stopped and yet another Select Committee formed to delve minutely into the methods of estimating and contracting. The Committee sat for the first session on March 3rd, 1831, and six further cross-examinations followed. James Pennethorne, Nash's trusted chief assistant and supervisor of so much of the London works, was there to give support. There was talk of Nash selling bricks from his own kiln at Norwood to contractors to his own advantage; tradesmen were examined to ascertain their relation with the architect; but after long and tedious probings, nothing bearing on financial connivance could be found and it remained for his professional competence in structural matters relating to the Palace to be tested before the inquisition was over. Nash's life-long rivals, the Attached Architects Soane and Smirke, together with Wyatville and Seward, Assistant Surveyor-General, were called in to report on the condition of the building, the claims of the tradesmen and how much money was needed to finish the work. After four months a report was delivered on July 15th, 1831, and Nash had to hear the humiliating criticisms of his work by those who, only a short while ago, had to recognise him (if not respect him) as the foremost architect in the land. They called in two engineers and an ironfounder and together they attempted to prove that Nash's construction of the Palace was at fault, especially where the use of iron girders was concerned.[1] The iron girders were proved to be entirely satisfactory and Nash's wrath at the whole procedure was demonstrated in a letter to the Committee:[2]

It must be obvious to everyone that the arrangement of the Plan and the Elevations of a Design have their origin in the *conveniences required*, and the *taste* of the Proprietor; and that it is the *province of the Architect* to *find the MEANS* of carrying them into effect; *thence* arose the construction in question—and it must be evident that if I had not had recourse to it, *I could not have given His Majesty the room he required*; the question I presume is, simply, whether the construction I have adopted renders the Building insecure; at present there are no appearances of weakness of any kind; they *insinuate*

[1] John U. Rastrick, an engineer, was in charge of testing Nash's use of iron.

[2] 1831 Select Committee, report on, App. XII, 1, p. 285.

weaknesses, but they *prove* none; nor *can they show any*, or *prove* that any additional security is required. I have said that none is required, and the Building is in every part perfectly secure; *and I call upon them to make any fair or just experiments they may think proper to justify the opinions they have given*; at present every part of their Report is founded on *conjecture*, on *opinions merely ASSERTED, not proved*; or where attempted to be founded on facts, *the facts STATED are NOT BORNE OUT.*

But the game was up; no one in authority had the slightest intention of retaining his services whether anything was proved or not. The Palace became the centre of derision and it was a popular blood-sport to suggest other names and uses for the building. These ranged from calling it the 'Brunswick Hotel'[1] to the suggestion that it should be turned into a laundry for half-pay officers.[2] In the summer of 1831, at the age of seventy-nine, Nash retreated to East Cowes and left the responsibility of supervising the remaining London improvements to Pennethorne. On the whole he emerged as a good loser especially as he had so much to lose; no architect had ever held so much power and responsibility, nor was one ever to do so again.

[1] *Creevey Papers*, 1905, p. 649. [2] Jekyll: *Letters*, p. 274.

CHAPTER EIGHT

Retreat to the South

AFTER his eclipse Nash made occasional visits to London from the Isle of Wight and travelled a little elsewhere to fulfil social and business engagements. A few weeks after the King's death he had even made a visit to Brighton and was seen with William IV in the grounds of the Pavilion,[1] perhaps making a gallant but pathetic attempt to re-establish royal favour before his final downfall.

The Palace was taken over by Edward Blore, but, as his predecessor was the only person who could possibly explain the complications of the work done there to date, Nash spent some time after his departure going over accounts and transactions with his own office staff.

Apart from 'dumb colic'[2] (possibly a 'grumbling' appendix) and recurrent costiveness, Nash had been a vigorous man, full of healthy energy and physical drive, matching his personality and innate optimism. But in 1830 he had suffered a stroke[3] that laid him up for eight months and from which he never fully recovered. From this moment onwards he must have started, as all old men do, to take stock of his life and the little personal incidents would have assumed, perhaps, more importance in his mind than the recent disagreeable months of inquisition. He may have remembered writing to his old friend, J. G. Philipps of Cwmgwili back in 1796, reminding him that his small son John, who was then in the Navy, was feeling homesick: 'You are a sad cold fellow ... none of you write to little John';[4] how Augustus Charles Pugin had thrived under his wing to become the most distinguished draughtsman of the day; how so many promising assistants from Pennethorne

[1] *Brighton Herald*, 21st August, 1830.
[2] Farington, entry for 5th November, 1821.
[3] 1831 Select Committee, report on, App. 1, 17, p. 72.
[4] Cwmgwili MSS.

to Burton had been loyal to him through all the years and how they themselves had prospered in their own fields. Such memories would be heightened by the death in 1833 of the mysterious friend or relation, John Edwards, his intimate from the earliest days.

In the spring of 1834 he wrote to the Office of Woods stating that he had left London for good and had assigned his practice to Pennethorne. To Alexander Milne[1] he wrote:

East Cowes Castle
March 22nd, 1834.

My dear Sir,

I have quitted London and resigned my Professional practice to Mr Pennethorne. I have deposited with him all my Papers, Plans and Designs of every kind relative to the Regents Park, New Street, Saint James's Park, Carlton House Terrace, and Buckingham House, and other matters connected with your Office in order that the Commissioners may have access to them, he being, as you know, as perfectly acquainted with every detail as I am myself, and in communicating this circumstance to your Board I beg most gratefully to thank them for every favor and indulgence which they have for so many years shown me, and I earnestly recommend Mr Pennethorne to their patronage, as perhaps the last act of kindness they can do me, and being well assured that he will acquit himself in all respects to my hope and to their satisfaction—and to say that if at any time my co-operation can be of use to their Board it will be most grateful to me to render it.

I have the honour to be
My dear Sir,
Your faithful Servant
John Nash.

Attached was a long list of plans, drawings and other documents concerning his London practice.[2]

His health was now rapidly deteriorating and in October of that year he made his will. After leaving legacies to friends, sisters-in-law and Edwards's widow, all real estate, after his wife's death, was to go to N. V. Edwards Vaughan, the son of his dead friend.

By the spring of 1835 Nash was bedridden, but still pleased to see visitors and his diary records his failing strength. On May 10th he wrote at Cowes: 'Very ill' and on 11th 'much worse'. Two days later he died and was buried in St James's churchyard next to the little Gothic church which he had designed in 1831. His tomb, of very simple sarcophagus shape, contrasts strangely with the fine marble mausoleum at Farningham in which rich Uncle Thomas was buried in 1778. The inscription reads:

[1] Official in the Office of Woods.

[2] A file copy of the list is in the possession of Mr Peter Silsby.

SACRED to the Memory of
JOHN NASH ESQ.re
Of East Cowes Castle:
who departed this life
May 13th, 1835
Aged 83 Years
ALSO, of MARY ANN his Wife
who died Febry 7th 1851
Aged 78 Years

His long and eventful life over, a final mystery accompanied his death. The money which he was to have left in his will, some £40,000, disappeared; he died in debt and East Cowes Castle and most of its contents were sold. His wife moved permanently to Hamstead where she remained with Anne and John Pennethorne until her death.

One hundred and thirty five years after his death, the name of Nash is more securely a part of the history of British architecture than ever. The obvious tribute to his talent was the decision not to destroy the Regent's Park terraces. But at the time his death passed almost unnoticed and the Annual Register of 1835 commented: 'As a speculative builder, this gentleman amassed a great fortune; but as an architect, he did not achieve anything that will confer upon him lasting reputation.' This ungenerous obituary, however, contrasted with appreciations from admirers and friends whose views coincided more nearly with ours of today. On May 18th of that year *John Bull* said:

> In private life Mr Nash was a warm and sincere friend; his mind active and comprehensive as it was, was singularly natural and simple; his conception was quick and clear; his thoughts were original, and his conversation was both instructive and pre-eminently agreeable.
>
> Look at the manner in which the interior of St James's Park was, in a few months, converted from a swampy meadow into a luxurious garden, and then, let the reader ask himself whether the metropolis is or is not indebted to the taste and genius of the much traduced object of this notice.

Nash's London architecture has never been much admired by those who analyse his designs, but even the most pedantic critic did not fail to recognise his brilliance in town-planning. In 1857 at a meeting of the Royal Institute of British Architects Nash's name came up and Mr William Tite (later Sir William), a prominent architect, said: 'Mr Nash had then succeeded Mr James Wyatt, who had been Surveyor-General, and although Mr Nash's style of architecture was anything but bold, his style of dealing with the improvements of the metropolis was so, and deserved the gratitude of this generation. . . .' At the same meeting C. R. Cockerell (second son of S. P. Cockerell) recorded: '. . . With all his defects, Nash was a courageous little man, and it was a matter of regret that no proper biography of him had appeared. . . .' James Pennethorne, to whom a gold medal was being presented at the meeting and who had to bear much of the adverse criticism of his late master's work '. . . wished to express his gratification at the remarks of the Chairman, Mr Tite, and Mr Cockerell, with reference to Mr Nash. There had been much difference of opinion with regard to the merit of that architect, and it was particularly agreeable to him, after a lapse of 30 years, to hear his works spoken of as they deserved. . . .' Later still, Edward M. Barry, Professor of Architecture at the Royal Academy, carried on the appreciation of Nash's planning ability (although he was critical of his buildings) in a lecture:[1]

> 'The first Gentleman in Europe' was contented with a seaside residence made up of pagodas and turrets, crowned with tee-totums and other details appropriate rather to a tea-garden than a royal palace, and Nash reigned supreme over London improvements.
>
> As I have mentioned Nash, it is only fair to say that as regards these improvements we owe him some thanks. He laid out Regent's street, from its commencement at Cockspur street, to its termination in Regent's Park. The architecture along this fine thoroughfare shows all the faults of the time, but the arrangement is managed with great skill, and any architect who may now be entrusted with similar work will find much to study with advantage in the plan of the successive squares, circuses, and curves which mark the disposition of the space. Taken altogether, I know of no such magnificent thoroughfare in any European city, if I except (and that only to a limited extent) the Boulevards of Paris. Nash's designs of the buildings are, as I have said, mean, and unworthy of their position; but this defect admits of improvement. The property on each side of the way belongs, I believe, to the Crown. We know what the present Duke of Westminster has done to Belgravia, and there is, therefore, a hope that some day a Minister of Works will be found who will perfect Nash's work, and make his own name illustrious, by compelling the erection of worthier architecture, and the substitution of stone and granite for the comp and lath-and-plaster shams of the Regency. When this has been done, and when the Thames Embankment has been properly completed and planted, London, already the most varied and picturesque of capitals, will have little to fear in the way of comparison.
>
> You must excuse this digression. I have made it, not only in justice to Nash, but because architects should have much to do in these days with Metropolitan improvements, and it is to be hoped they may be marked with the same breadth and boldness of plan shown by him. . . .

[1] At the Royal Academy, 12th March, 1874.

Charles James Mathews,[1] father of an erstwhile pupil of Nash, used the vexed word 'genius' in his appraisal of his son's old master:[2] '. . . his genius lying less in Classical detail than in bold conception and general arrangement. . . .' Nearer to our own times the word has been given a sterner meaning and Sir Edwin Lutyens, when writing of Philip Webb's talent in 1915, said: 'I did not recognise it then to be the internal youth of genius, though it was conjoined with another attribute of genius—thoroughness!'[3] Of all Nash's attributes thoroughness was not one; careful detailing was almost always sacrificed to the total effect. The work for which he is most remembered represents the dying-fall of Classicism, the high Indian Summer of a long tradition. Not one of his London buildings would stand comparison with the epic architecture of St Petersburg or Paris. Nash produced something far less splendid, but utterly suited to London and its times. He was essentially a 'man of the times', being able to see at once the broad problems involved. Moreover he had the drive and enough talent to grapple with them; thus his temperament was perfectly matched to his task. Had he been intellectual and scholarly his output might have been dimmed, his adventurous spirit inhibited. Many men of exceptional creative ability are two people: the artist and the man; but Nash the artist was also Nash the man and every aspect of his life bore this out.

An assessment of Nash's contribution to architecture, however, cannot rest only on his achievements as a town-planner; they represent the final challenge to a man nearing sixty, landscaping the urban scene in the idiom of the day with zest, even impatience. When he started this great undertaking, he had already built over forty country houses and many public buildings and it is to these country houses that we must return—to the quieter days of his early and middle life—in order to see Nash the architect. Here again he was working in the idiom of the day, but with more opportunity to express himself freely with imagination and wit. If he never evolved an intensely personal style there are some common threads of invention that link those early houses; and if some of them are more interesting than others, there are ones that alone would secure him an elevated place in the history of the English house.

In his work, as in his life, there were brilliant moments. The broad picture of his achievements is often lost in the pedantic search for perfect detail, although, some forty years before his birth, Alexander Pope had challenged such ideals when he wrote:

Most Critics, fond of some subservient art,
Still make the Whole depend upon a Part.
They talk of principles, but notions prize,
And all to one lov'd Folly sacrifice.

[1] *See* p. 22. [2] C. J. Mathews: *op. cit.*
[3] Christopher Hussey: *Life of Sir Edwin Lutyens*, 1953, p. 26.

List of Executed Works

Aberystwyth Bridge, Cards. *c.* 1798. Replaced in 1886.

Abergavenny Market, Mon. 1795. *See* p. 20.

Albury, Surrey, date unknown. Bridge for Samuel Thornton, no longer existing.

All Souls', Langham Place, London. 1822. *See* p. 73.

Aqualate Hall, Staffs. 1808. For Sir John F. Boughey, Bt. *See* p. 41.

Ascot, Royal Stand. 1821. For George IV, since demolished.

Attingham Park, Shropshire. *c.* 1810. For Lord Berwick; alterations and additions. *See* p. 42.

Bank Farm, Kingston-on-Thames. *c.* 1796. For Major-General St John, since demolished.

Barnsley Park, Gloucs. 1806–10. For J. Musgrave; additions and decorations. *See* p. 37.

Blaise Hamlet and Blaise Castle, Gloucs. Cottages for J. S. Harford, 1811; conservatory, *c.* 1803. *See* p. 37.

Bloomsbury Square. *c.* 1778. Nash's own property; altered but still existing. *See* p. 17.

Brighton, Royal Pavilion. 1815–23. For the Prince Regent. *See* p. 83 et seq.

Buckingham Palace. 1825–30. For George IV. *See* p. 93 et seq.

Bulstrode. *c.* 1800. For the Duke of Portland; alterations not now existing.

Caerhayes Castle, Cornwall. *c.* 1808. For J. Trevanion. *See* p. 41.

Caledon, Co. Tyrone. *c.* 1812. For 2nd Earl of Caledon; alterations and additions. *See* p. 52.

Cardigan Gaol. 1793. Demolished. *See* p. 19.

Cardigan Priory. *c.* 1792. For Thomas Johnes, father of Johnes of Hafod; much altered to form hospital.

Carlton House, London. 1813. For the Prince Regent; alterations and decorations, since demolished. *See* pp. 80–81.

Carlton House Terrace, London. 1827. For the Crown. *See* p. 80.

Carmarthen Gaol. 1789–92. Demolished 1938. *See* p. 19.

Carmarthen: Green Gardens. *c.* 1785. *See* p. 18.

Casina, Dulwich. 1797. For Richard Shawe. *See* p. 35.

Castle House, Aberystwyth. *c.* 1793? For Uvedale Price. *See* p. 23.

Chichester, Market House. 1807. Altered.

Childwall Hall, Lancs. *c.* 1806. For Bamber Gascoyne, M.P., since demolished. *See* p. 39.

Clarence House, St James's. 1825. For the Duke of Clarence; remodelled 1873. *See* p. 93.

Corsham Court, Wilts. 1797. For P. C. Methuen, with John Adey Repton; additions and alterations. *See* p. 36.

County Fire Office, London. 1819. For the Crown; with Robert Abraham, since demolished. *See* p. 76.

Cronkhill, Shropshire. *c.* 1802. For Lord Berwick. *See* p. 42.

Derryloran, parish church, Cookstown, Co. Tyrone. 1822. *See* p. 51.

Dolaucothi, Carmarthenshire. 1792–95. For John Johnes; alterations, now in ruins. *See* p. 22.

Dover Street, No 29. *c.* 1799. Nash's own house, since demolished. *See* p. 59.

East Cowes Castle, Isle of Wight. From 1798. Nash's own house, since demolished and site developed. *See* p. 60.

East Cowes Church (St James's). 1831. *See* p. 101.

Ffynone, Pembs. 1793. For Capt. Colby. *See* p. 25.

Foley House, Haverfordwest, Pembs. 1793. For Richard Foley. *See* p. 29.

Garnstone, Herefords. *c.* 1806. For Samuel Peploe, since demolished. *See* p. 39.

Golden Grove, Carmarthen. 1787. Bathroom for John Vaughan, since demolished. *See* p. 22.

Gracefield Lodge, Co. Kildare. 1817. For Mrs Kavanagh. *See* p. 54.

Hafod, Cardigans. 1793. For Col Thomas Johnes; alterations and additions, now in ruins. *See* p. 22.

Hale Hall, Lancs. *c.* 1806. For John Blackburne, M.P.; south front, since demolished.

Hamstead, Isle of Wight. *c.* 1803. Nash's own country house, since rebuilt. *See* p. 61.

Haymarket Theatre, London. 1820. *See* p. 80.

Hereford Gaol. 1796. Demolished. *See* p. 19.

Highgate Hill Tunnel. 1813. For Highgate Archway Co.; construction of viaduct, demolished 1901.

High Legh, Cheshire. *c.* 1806. For George John Legh; interior fittings, cottages, farm buildings, etc.

Hillgrove, Bembridge, Isle of Wight. *c.* 1814. For the Earl of Ducie, now in disrepair. *See* p. 62.

Hollycombe, Hants. *c.* 1800. For Charles Taylor, since rebuilt. *See* p. 38.

Ingestre Hall, Staffs. Undated. For Lord Talbot; restoration, later burnt in 1882.

Isle of Wight, Market and Guildhall. 1814. Isle of Wight Institution. 1811. *See* p. 62.

Kentchurch Court, Herefordshire. *c.* 1795. For John Scudamore; Gothic remodelling.

Killymoon Castle, Co. Tyrone. *c.* 1802. For Colonel William Stewart, M.P. *See* p. 44 et seq.

Kilwaughter Castle, Co. Antrim. 1807. For Edward Jones Agnew; now in ruins. *See* p. 51.

King's Opera House, London. 1820. For the Crown; rebuilt 1893. *See* p. 80.

Kingston House, London. Undated. For Lord Listowel; alterations, since demolished.

Knepp Castle, Sussex. 1809. For Sir Charles Burrell, Bt. *See* p. 40.

Lissan Rectory, Co. Tyrone. 1807. For the Rev. John Staples. *See* p. 52.

Llanayron, Aberayron. *c.* 1794. For Major Lewis. *See* p. 28.

Llysnewydd, Cardiganshire. *c.* 1794. For Colonel Lewes. *See* p. 27.

Longner Hall, Shropshire. 1806. For Robert Burton. *See* p. 39.

Lough Cutra Castle, Co. Galway. Before 1817. For Charles Vereker, M.P. *See* p. 55.

Luscombe Castle, Devon. *c.* 1800. For Charles Hoare. *See* p. 36.

Marble Arch, London. 1829. For George IV. *See* p. 95.

Merly House, Dorset. Undated. For Mr Willett; stables.

Moccas Court, Herefordshire. *c.* 1805. For Sir George Cornewall; lodges and cottages.

Ophthalmic Hospital, Albany Street, London. 1818. Nash's own speculation, since demolished. *See* p. 70.

Parnham, Dorset. *c.* 1810. For Sir W. Oglander; Gothic additions.

Picton Monument, Carmarthen. 1825. Demolished. *See* p. 26.

Preshaw House, Hampshire. 1810. For W. Long; Gothic additions.

Ravensworth Castle, Co. Durham. 1808. For Sir Thomas Liddell, since demolished. *See* p. 41.

Regent's Canal, London. 1820 (opened). *See* p. 68.

Regent's Park, London. From 1812. For the Crown. *See* p. 63 et seq.

Regent Street, London. From 1817. For the Crown. *See* p. 72 et seq.

Rheola, Neath. *c.* 1812. For John Edwards; enlargement of small house.

Rockingham, Co. Roscommon. 1810. For Lord Lorton of Boyle; since burnt down. *See* p. 53.

Royal Lodge (The King's Cottage), Windsor. 1814. For George IV; rebuilt. *See* p. 81.

St David's Cathedral, Pembrokeshire. 1793. West front; now replaced. *See* p. 20.

St James's Palace, London. 1821. For the Crown; state rooms. *See* p. 81.

St James's Park, London. 1814 and later. For the Crown; laying out and temporary buildings. *See* p. 81.

St Mary's, Haggerston, London. 1826. Destroyed by bombs, 1940.

St Peter's, Carmarthen. *c.* 1786. Repairs to roof; collapsed 1860. *See* p. 17.

Sandridge Park, Devon. 1805. For Lady Ashburton. *See* p. 42.

Shanbally Castle, Co. Tipperary. *c.* 1812. For the Earl of Lismore, since demolished. *See* p. 54.

Shane's Castle, Co. Antrim. *c.* 1812. For Earl O'Neill, since burnt down. *See* p. 51.

Sion House, Tenby. *c.* 1790. For William Routh, since burnt down. *See* p. 24.

Someries House, Regent's Park, London. Demolished. *See* p. 70.

Southborough Place, Surrey. 1808. For Thomas Langley. *See* pp. 30, 42.

Southgate Grove, London. 1797. For Walker Gray. *See* p. 35.

Stanford Bridge, Worcestershire. 1795. For Sir Edward Winnington. *See* p. 21.

Suffolk Street, London. 1820. For the Crown. *See* p. 79.

Sundridge Park, Kent. 1799. For Claude Scott; altered. *See* p. 36.

Temple Druid, Pembrokeshire. *c.* 1796. For H. Bulkeley. *See* p. 30.

United Service Club, London. 1828. *See* p. 81.

Uppark, Sussex. Undated. *c.* 1800. For Sir H. Fetherstonhaugh; alterations.

Waterloo Place. From 1815. For the Crown. *See* p. 76.

West Cowes, Gothic villa. *c.* 1825. For Sir J. Coxe Hippisley, since altered.

West Cowes Church. 1816. For G. Ward; mausoleum tower.

West Grinstead Park, Sussex. *c.* 1806. For Walter Burrell, now in ruins. *See* p. 39.

Whitson Court, Newport, Mon. *c.* 1795. For W. Phillips. *See* p. 31.

Windsor Castle. *c.* 1830. Pedestal for statue of George III for the Park.

Witley Court, Worcs. *c.* 1805. For Lord Foley; alterations. *See* p. 73.

Unless otherwise stated, dates refer to commencement of building.

This list does not include projects often exhibited at the Royal Academy during Nash's life—numerous cottages, stables and other small buildings for Royal Parks and Forests and for Repton's and Nash's clients. George Stanley Repton's Notebooks contain many designs for these small buildings and some are listed in Summerson: *op. cit.* and H. M. Colvin: *Biographical Dictionary of English Architects.*

Works Attributed to Nash

Aberayron, Cardiganshire, *c.* 1808. Replanning and development. *See* p. 31.
Cahir, Co. Tipperary, Protestant church. Undated.
Colby Lodge, Tenby. Undated. For the Colby family.
Farningham. 1778. Mausoleum. *See* p. 16.
Hopton Court, Shropshire. *c.* 1812. Additions.
Jeremy's Hotel, Carmarthen. *c.* 1786. *See* p. 18.
Kildress Church, Co. Tyrone. Ceiling. *See* p. 51.
Monachty, near Aberayron. *c.* 1808. For Rev. Gwynne. *See* p. 31.
St. Mary's Isle, Kirkcudbright. *c.* 1796. For Lord Selkirk; cottage and mausoleum. *See* p. 38.
Six Bells, Carmarthen. *c.* 1786. *See* p. 18.
Stonelands, Dawlish, Devon. For the Hoare family. *See* p. 37.
St. David's Church, Carmarthen. Built to Nash's designs after his death?

Further Reading

Angus, W. 'Seats of the Nobility and Gentry', 1797.
Bolton, A. T. 'The Portrait of Sir John Soane', 1927.
Brayley, E. W. 'Her Majesty's Palace at Brighton', 1838.
Britton, J. & Pugin, A. 'Illustrations of the Public Buildings of London', 1825-27.
Clark, K. 'The Gothic Revival', 1928, revised edition 1964.
Colvin, H. M. 'Biographical Dictionary of English Architects', 1954.
Croly, G. 'Personal History of George IV', 1841.
Davis, T. 'The Architecture of John Nash', 1960.

Dickens, C. (ed), 'The Life of Charles James Matthews', 1879.
Eastlake, C. L. 'A History of the Gothic Revival', 1872 (reprinted with new introduction by J. M. Crook, 1970).
Elmes, J. 'Metropolitan Improvements', 1828.
Farington, J. 'Diary' (Ed. J. Grieg) 1922-28.
Fulford, R. 'George IV', 1949.
Harris, J. 'Buckingham Palace' (The Architecture), 1968.
Harwood, T. E. ' Windsor Old and New', 1929.
Hussey, C. 'The Picturesque', 1927, reprinted 1967.
Hussey, C. 'Country Life', (various articles).
Hussey, C. 'English Country Houses', Late Georgian, 1958.
Hussey, C. 'English Country Houses', Mid-Georgian, 1956.
Irwin, D. 'English Neoclassical Art', 1961.
Knight, R. P. 'The Landscape', 1794.
Loudon, J. C. '. . . the Landscape Architecture of the late Humphry Repton', 1840.
Morshead, O. 'George IV and Royal Lodge', 1965.
Musgrave, C. 'Royal Pavilion . . .', 1959.
Neale, J. P. 'Views of the Seats of Noblemen and Gentlemen . . .', 1818-29.
Pevsner, N. 'An Outline of European Architecture', 1943.
Pevsner, N. 'The Buildings of England' (various vols from 1951).
Pilcher, D. 'The Regency Style', 1946.
Pyne, W. H. 'Royal Residences', 1819.
Robinson, C. J. 'The Mansions of Herefordshire . . .', 1873.
Rowe, T. ' Westmorland, Cumberland, Durham and Northumberland', 1832.
Saunders, A. 'Regent's Park', 1969.
Sichel, W. (ed), 'The Glenbervie Journals', 1811.
Smith, H. Clifford. 'The Complete History of Buckingham Palace', 1930.
Spencer, H. 'London's Canal', 1961.
Stroud, D. 'Humphry Repton', 1962.
Summerson, J. 'John Nash', 1935, reprinted 1949.
Summerson, J. 'Georgian London', 1945, revised edition 1963.
Summerson, J. 'Architecture in Britain', 1953.
Summerson, J. 'Heavenly Mansions', 1949.
Turnor, R. 'The Smaller English House', 1952.
Watkin, D. 'Thomas Hope', 1968.

Index

Figures in parenthesis refer to plate and figure numbers